ALLEYN

BELLEFLEUR

BOISVERT

GAGNON

GAUCHER

GOULET

HURTUBISE

JAQUE

LEDUC

LEMIEUX

LETENDRE

MOLINARI

PELLAN

RIOPELLE

TONNANCOUR

TOUSIGNANT

This publication was produced by the
Vie des Arts Society thanks to the assistance of the
Imperial Oil Company Limited.
Executive Director, Andrée Paradis.
Artistic Director, Claude Beaulieu.
Executive Editor, Jules Bazin.
Art Production and Design, Gilles Gourdeau.
Translation, Mildred Grand, Eithne Bourget and
Joan Thornley.
Distribution, Christiane Haxaire.

Jacket
Design, Gilles Gourdeau.
Photography, Jean-Pierre Beaudin.

Table of Contents

Preface

This is the first volume in a series we have titled *A Survey of Creators*. Thanks to the generous participation of the Imperial Oil Company, *Vie des Arts* is in a position to produce a project that has been dear to our hearts for a long time: to cast, with the help of a publication more permanent than a periodical, new light on artists of our time, by showing their ways of living and working. What the artists are coincides with their creation. But their work also harmonizes with their manner of creating, with their immediate environment, with all that weaves the web of everyday life, with constant immersion in the interior world.

Our goal in calling upon the double testimony of the photographer and the writer was simple: to foster comprehension through the eye and to give free rein to the interpretive premises that have the works as object.

We asked our photographers to capture the artist in his studio, in his home, in his moments of relaxation, in some of his habits, convinced in advance that our hunters of images would bring revealing snapshots, each in his own way. Each photographer has his own approach, his style. As things developed, it became evident that each has, besides, his own ways of persuasion, the artist being easily rebellious at any intrusion into his personal life.

We also invited sixteen art critics and historians to present the painters dealt with in the present volume, leaving them free to treat their subject as they saw fit. Some remained faithful to their own method of analysis: others were more interested in the human side of the experiment. From this variety of interpretation, from these ideas and these images, from this meeting of writer and photographer, there results a living document that speaks to us of artists who all have in common the circumstance of having been born in Quebec, even if they live in Toronto or Paris. These creators draw inspiration from the same source, their roots are in the same soil, they live in their work. It is not necessary here to seek an historical perspective or a classification in order of importance; other volumes will come, as eloquent in their choice. It is the unique feature of each artistic experiment that interests us.

To see the world with the eyes of the artist is a way of loving without possessing, it is to share a vision that goes always further, that tries constantly to force back the barriers of ignorance. The artist teaches us the world because he does not rest until he has exhausted all resources, that is to say almost never.

It is easy to feel in the pages that follow how much familiar surrounding things are a source of wonder for him. Affectionate relationships are established with the most humble objects, with landscapes, with close persons. But it is still in action, at his easel, that the artist best reveals himself. There the process of creation finds its outcome and, as the creator does not know this kind of respite, he remains to the end prisoner of his interrogations, his anguish, his hopes.

Let the pleasure of the eye open new horizons for us and, especially, let it bring us close to a world where art is born. Where living forces dwell, and vitality. Art is a matter of the senses, of the mind, and the eye leads us toward unexplored regions.

Andrée PARADIS

ALLEYN

Florence de MÈREDIEU

*For us excess is only a hideous sign,
reminding us ceaselessly that death,
a break in this individual discontinuity
to which anguish rivets us, is offered to us
as a truth more eminent than life.*
(Georges Bataille)

*Men are becoming the transistors in an
immense circuit.*

(Marshall McLuhan)

One might say of Alleyn's work that it dwells in our reality, that of everyday life, the universe of the media and consumption, a reality perceived through certain hallucinations coming back across the work in a haunting fashion; sun, time and death. Doubtless it is there that one must locate the universe suited to Alleyn, a planet to be situated somewhere between McLuhan and Bataille.

The figures painted in acrylic and then in oil on transparent plexiglass panels and arranged as in everyday life but also under another aspect, as in a museum, facing canvases representing a series of setting suns, form a key moment in Alleyn's work, in the sense that they put into play certain significant ruptures. A rupture first of all with a certain system of the presentation of works of art: *Une belle fin de journée* functions as a parody of a museum: fake figures contemplating in front of fake canvases, a poor replica — as Yves Robillard points out — of the cyclorama device. Artificial décors, papier mâché figures examined minutely and scrupulously in all their details, unreal acid colours, reality made up like the postcards of yesterday. The museum's eventual visitors themselves combine with the exhibition by blending into the mass of painted figures. Alleyn confesses that, in the galleries, he often looks, not at the exhibition, but at the persons who are looking at it "as if the people were exhibited works". Again a rupture with a formalist and abstract painting in which form and structure alone are of importance. From this arises the irony of the sunset shown in Mondrian's canvas, this elitist style of painting appearing as passé. "Little by little," says Alleyn, "contemporary life has entered into my work, and this is what feeds it much more than aesthetic theories." After the series of objects that resulted in the creation of *Introscaphe* (1970), a work that represents a return to painting but also a desire to transcend painting by going beyond the pictorial wall in two dimensions, incapable by itself alone to render an account of the polyphony of sensations that assail man in his everyday life.

Therefore it is a matter of bringing to an end the involvement with a certain idea of style in painting or in art, and, in so doing, of running the risk of again becoming narrative; of daring the commonplace, the trite, the everyday. This wish to escape established cultural routes through the creation of environments and structures directly integrated into the urban fabric already subtended the production of *Introscaphe,* originally conceived to function in the subway or a shopping centre. This concern for integration finds its most accomplished expression in an ensemble the painter is presently producing for a public building at Sept-Isles: the full-length portrait of some twelve of its inhabitants will be reproduced on glass panels and placed in front of canvases illustrating the town's history. Past and present, art and reality will be mingled, then confronted with the progressive wear of time.

Alleyn does not conceal the difficulty that exists in again becoming figurative. This involves re-learning to read and especially to *transcribe* a reality offered in all its existential density, and one would wish to take it just as it is to set it intact on the canvas like those transfers whose actual drawing, prefabricated, is revealed only on the paper. There the rôle of the photographic medium occurs, as does the use of the different media (television, picture-stories, etc.) which come close to reality at the same time as they banish it; the painter, in fact, works not on reality but on an intermediary language conveying and transposing the aforesaid reality. The influence of the media is such to-day, besides, that they form — as McLuhan explains — an organic and mental function just as does breathing or thinking. Even erotism is hemmed in and coloured by advertising and the media. In *Intérieur* (1969), two kinds of reality are superposed and clash with each other: a blurred view as in filigree of a couple making love; background and section of the typical apartment for a young, dynamic executive.

Alert to the possibilities of cinema and video, Alleyn conceived *Une belle fin de journée* as a film-strip, a succession of snapshots that set the figures. The production of the work is supported on photographs made at La Ronde in 1973-1974. The painting is, however, not a copy of the photograph, in any case; the latter could prove deficient in its purely representative function. Alleyn then has recourse to palliatives, has models pose to complete the photographic reproduction, combines, invents images. Photography therefore takes the place of a simple instrument to oust reality.

Contrary to many hyperrealists, it is not the object that is at the centre of the artist's preoccupations, but the human being. An obsession with faces, bodies and attitudes which sometimes speak more surely than faces, an obsession with clothing, with all this jumble of accessories that acts like a prothesis for us. And, nevertheless, its figures are seen as objects, *fixed*. The cold chamber of the consumer society where the merchandise is the humans themselves frozen in their most everyday and most prosaic manners of being. The man-machine of the period of *Agressions* and *Conditionnements* still knew — in spite of the icy, mechanical order with which it was faced — the breakdown and the orgasmic laceration that reassured man on his account by showing him that pain is irreducible to technological order. In spite of its wheels, pistons, nozzles, borers, computers and anatomical boards, the mechanical universe did not appear closed. A break in the order could happen. The bursting of the human module produced smudges, rents that were not possible to assimilate in the mechanical order where they occurred.

In 1974's works, on the contrary, the death operation was accomplished in an odourless and callous manner: man is no longer anything more than dead, frozen meat on the butcher's stand in the consumer society. This clearly appears in the project of a *Museum of Consumerism* with which Alleyn is playing and would consist of fixing and freezing in place a whole complex of stores and supermarkets, the people standing like statues while preserving the shortlived attitude they held at the moment when everything was interrupted. We could, Alleyn thinks, replace the merchandise according to the seasons, but the persons would not change and he adds, "Fixed in this way in time and space, container and contents will become at the same time museum and museological objects presented henceforth to the studious curiosity of our descendants". The shopping centre, a perfect symbol of the consumer society, betrays the death-dealing character of our neo-capitalist societies that kill, freeze, conserve and consume.

The plexiglass surfaces on which the figures of *Une belle fin de journée* are painted act from this point of view like cellophane envelopes, automatic wrappings of frozen products. A transparent sarcophagus in which individuals are enclosed, exposed and visible, dead and artificial as in their lives. In this way a zone of illusion and phantasm is marked out, space and the negation of space at the same time, a dead zone indicated as such. No man's land by which Alleyn breaks away from photorealism to reach a surrealism of everyday life where banality and vulgarity acquire a cosmic dimension. Art is not a second reality to be developed; it is already there in the form of ready-made products for the consumer society. Likewise the museum that could "preserve the memory of this insatiable appetite"; this museum "is within reach of our will, not in the form of an empty shell patiently waiting for the slow accumulation of the fruits of toilsome excavations, but already existing, already filled with treasures we do not recognize as such." Here Alleyn's painting reflects the evolution of the sociological context in which it is anchored. Vertigo and agony, but also attraction with regard to technological progress and its repercussions on everyday life of the sixties, have made place for a real nausea in the face of the insatiable hyperconsumerism of a society whose greatest problem is to absorb the flood of useless merchandise it produces: "The Consumer Era. This is certainly the way that the future will designate the period in which we presently live in North America. What activity other than consumption includes and synthesizes so well the most characteristic aspects of our civilization?"

Neither photorealist nor hyperrealist, Alleyn's work arises rather from what might be called *pararealism*: invention and the pursuit of nested parallel realities, twin sisters of reality but subtly shifted, moved out of place by superposition, redundancies, echoes, mirror effects, clever, carefully proportioned illusions. Alleyn's last drawings are similar, in this line, to *art-fiction*: invention of spaces and impossible temporalities, omnipresence of figures, transplanted grafted spaces, time spiralling and turning back on itself. The multiplication and interference of different orders of reality, deliberately maintained ambiguity, the imperceptible slipping of the virtual image toward the real image, give rise to the fact that one never knows if the image functions as a model or as a double, as a reflection or as a reality. The mechanisms of dreams (as Freud described them) play fully here through condensation, displacement, crystallization of images and figures, and one would wish to be able to speak of plays on images as of plays on words.

Some of these drawings invoke a quasi-photographic, indeed even cinematographic, reading. Use of negatives, masks, repetition and film distortion of the image, which sufficiently reveals the obsession of a frozen time, a constant obsession in all Alleyn's work: *"Une belle fin de journée* is a meditation on the memory of the visible, on the times that superimpose themselves, a see-saw motion between a mental space and a physical one, a transition in abeyance (. . .) I try to endow emotion with a memory." As if from the only sedimented accumulation of mnemonic layers — and by means of voyeuristic fascination — there could arise a representative image of death and its temporal substitutes. This archaelogical dimension of memory (cf. *Cool Control*, 1968) allows us to understand this phenomenon on *self-quotation* that is so frequent in Alleyn's work. And this is true of the canvas titled $X =$, which should be considered as a lexicon of all his works.

Everywhere associated with death, sometimes haunted by a Pekin man skeleton, the sunset is one of the fundamental elements in Alleyn's basic vocabulary. A dying sun in which Freud and Bataille would have seen a symbol of castration, orgasmic and solar castration. Often represented in a round cartouche, joined with water and femininity, it displays a phantasm of regression already present at the production of *Introscaphe*. "It is not without a reason that the object is ovoid, thus placing the participant in an enclosure that brings him back to the origins of life. A reassuring form, an archetypal form, not transferable. But remembering as well cosmic vessels, flight-objects of contemporary mythology." In this closed universe, the evacuation of impulse is carried on by compulsive, syncopated repetition, which explains why the movement in Alleyn's work is everywhere fixed, taken at the moment, arrested and frozen. A codified movement purely mechanical in the series *Agressions* and *Conditionnements*, anonymity and mysterious opacity of the figures, such as this woman seen from the back that he decided not to show from all sides as Picasso did, but immobile and fixed in a transitory attitude. Fixity, like death, makes things final by proposing a type of *other* possession, breaking with the absurd production-consumption cycle.

Where Freud would have unmasked the tricks of the death wish working silently in Eros, life and death exchange their characteristics: life is only decrepitude, destruction and the consuming of perishable property, a dead life rotten at the core. Death, on the contrary, by fixing and freezing living beings, immortalizes and renders invulnerable to time.

12

EDMUND ALLEYN   BIOGRAPHICAL NOTES

Edmund Alleyn was born at Quebec in 1931. A graduate of the Montreal School of Fine Arts, in 1955 he received the Grand Prize of the Artistic Competitions of the Province of Quebec. Four years later, he won a bronze medal at the São Paulo Biennial. In 1970, the French Television Office produced a colour film on Edmund Alleyn and his audio-visual sculpture, *Introscaphe*. In 1971, after living several years in Paris, Alleyn returned to Quebec. He has been teaching at the Visual Arts Department of the University of Ottawa since 1972.

SELECTED BIBLIOGRAPHY

1956   Marjorie Masson, *The Edmund Alleyn Show*, at Arvida, in *Vie des Arts*, Vol. I, No. 2, p. 25.

1960   Pierre Courthion, *Alleyn*, in *Vie des Arts*, Vol. IV, No. 18, p. 25-29.

1964   Michel Beaulieu, *Edmund Alleyn*, in *Vie des Arts*, Vol. IX, No. 37, p. 51.

1966   *Edmund Alleyn*. Introduction by Denys Chevalier, Galerie Édouard Smith, Paris.

1967   *Edmund Alleyn: Conditionnement*. Introduction by Gérald Gassiot-Talabot; Poem by
          Michel Butor; Galerie Blumenthal-Mommaton, Paris.
       Yvon Taillandier, *Edmund Alleyn: L'Angoisse de l'an 2000*, in *Connaissance des Arts*, No. 182.
       Yves Robillard, *De l'homme, des schémas et des machines*, in *La Presse*, Montreal, November 4.

1970   Jean Clair, *Interview with Edmund Alleyn*, in *Chroniques de l'Art Vivant*, No. 14.

1971   Jean-René Ostiguy, *Un siècle de peinture canadienne*. Laval University Press, Quebec.

1974   Guy Robert, *Alleyn*, in *Vie des Arts*, Vol. XIX, No. 75, pp. 12-16.
       Georges Bogardi, *Edmund Alleyn at the Museum of Contemporary Art*, in *The Montreal Star*,
          October 19, p. D-10.
       Gilles Toupin, *Edmund Alleyn: Un drop-out made in Québec*, in *La Presse*, October 19.

1975   Paul Dumas, *Une belle fin de journée* with Edmund Alleyn at the Quebec Museum and the Museum
          of Contemporary Art, in *L'Information médicale et paramédicale*, February 4.

BELLEFLEUR

Guy ROBERT

Giving to see, Éluard said of poetry. Showing, we generally say of painting. With regard to Léon Bellefleur, and to attempt to *see* his work to a small extent according to the exact nature of his reality, it would be necessary to avoid these "manipulations of the intellect" which Carlos Castaneda feared, and to try rather to follow a very different route, apart from all the more or less recent styles, those of Marxist sociology, psychoanalytical grids or rabid semiology; leaving these styles to jostle each other and to wear themselves out, I prefer to rely on certain aesthetic facts like those complementary ones of polysemiology and polymorphism in works of art, to propose, regarding Léon Bellefleur's work itself, the approach of esoterism, seldom employed until now concerning this artist who has been fed on it, nonetheless, for a third of a century.

Léon the Hermit

The magic scrawls that Bellefleur has been drawing and painting for so many years catch the eye with their fascinating signals; and, during the many seasons I have known him, I have often heard Léon begin certain sentences with "You see . . ." half questioning, as if in this way he were sounding, with the end of the word, the availability of his interlocutor, his state of clairvoyance, his esoteric coefficient.

Seeing. Seeing that everything that goes on and is connected, that all is sign and that the whole universe constantly makes signs to us, that all hermetism is such only for the blind or for those who will not see, since it is half-open.

Léon Bellefleur's gaze is what I first noticed about him already twenty years ago. A light glance, a bit dreamy, perhaps absent-minded, but distracted by what? By what veil, what secret is it clouded?

And Bellefleur's work. A varied work, composed of paintings, drawings and prints. A veiled work, like the gaze from which it is born, a secret work in some way occult.

Occult? Yes, in part, surely, and thus by this fact half-open, murmuring; varied, by all evidence, and yet so well attuned to itself and faithful to the profound internal breath that inspires it and that it expresses and encodes.

And the gaze goes from the man to his work, in a patient back and forth movement; for this is neither the time nor the place to attack, to force the door that is obviously hidden. One must know how to let this come by itself; and slowly, gently, cautiously, the scene becomes clear, never flooded with light; with Bellefleur, one would say that it is never noon; there is always some shadow that indicates the direction of the light toward the realm it could not enter and which it is content to leave to be guessed all around: the kingdom of the unknown.

Léon the Hermit. The ninth of the twenty-two major cards in the Book of Thoth, the ninth tarot arcana comes into view, and it is this image that Léon Bellefleur holds out to me by way of identity card, a portrait in code; the icon of the bearded Hermit, in the big red mantle lined with blue, holding a rod and a lantern on a dark background.

Léon the Hermit, perfectly attuned to the quiet life in the village of Saint-Antoine-sur-le-Richelieu, where he has been living for some years with his wife, Rita, between the calm river and the long lands of the back country. Also, near the Richelieu, the light spreads out and the air is velvety. We speak softly, as if not to disturb the order of the four Elements whose staircase Homer — Bachelard — would doubtless have been enchanted to climb, a staircase leading to the artist's studio in the attic.

Here the beams are within reach of the hand, the slope of the roof within reach of light, the work within reach of the heart. On a wooden table the arcana of the Tarot of Marseilles are carefully laid out in two rows, beside notes that the artist has written for me, which describe his development in a view in which "painting and magic are always linked", in which "the pictorial adventure is a continual quest", in which André Breton is beside Éliphas Lévi in accordance with a "chain of analogies" that does not fail to reveal an esoteric subsoil in Dante.

The painter stretches out his hand toward the table, hesitates, takes the Hermit, comments on the card, hinting. Because the Arcana IX does not speak up, he confides; rather, and is always a little suspicious. According to Oswald Wirth's commentaries, inspired by the sealed tradition synthesized by Lévi and Stanislas de Guaita, the Arcana of the Hermit is entered in a "cosmogonic sketch" following which "an invisible creation precedes the one that falls under the senses[1]: the mysterious artist who dreams up the types appears in Tarot in the guise of the Hermit, weaver of the permanent, unsubstantial web upon which is embroidered the transitory representation of appearances"; the "initiative programme" of this Hermit could be summed up in the concentration of the faculties, thanks to isolation and to silence, until the path which is to be followed appears, with caution but without retreat; in the light of hermetic philosophy, the Hermit unfolds into an experienced Adept, whose research avoids becoming dull in the maze of material things, the better to devote himself to the search of the spirit.

The Game and the Quest

And let the unbeliever not take it into his head to desecrate all this, let him simply go on his way, since the Hermit has not even felt the non-existence of such a being without shadow and without play; because it is a game that is involved (and let the serious abstain from it!) in Tarot, as has been seen by Roger Caillois, who, after all, is not a mere nobody in matters of art and aesthetics: "So the game is a microcosm, an alphabet of emblems, that covers the universe"[2].

A long association with Léon Bellefleur's work uncovers exactly this playful alphabet, in the form of a glossary or rather a series of symbols, hieroglyphic signs, cryptograms that offer to the imagination and the vision fruitful but untranslatable trails in logical and univocal formulas.

Other artists produce pictures that words succeed in better encompassing; but when facing the works of artists like Bellefleur one must first consent to wander in the gardens of analogy and ambiguity, as far as misunderstanding. Let us not fall into error for all that, however: to call Tarot to mind in the face of Léon the Hermit has nothing to do with chronicles of horoscopes or talking tables; Tarot appears because it is image and bridge in this studio between the alchemist's laboratory and the monk's chapel; it is certainly Art that it always involves, the Great Art of metamorphosis, the Great Work of the Quest, a Way similar to that of the millenary Chinese Tao suggesting the intuition of A Total in the hermetic gnosis by which the microcosm of human awareness and universal macrocosm correspond.

The Quest. This word returns to punctuate painter Bellefleur's conversations, like the word "fervour" that he is fond of, in the most intense moments, at the densest turning-points, at the most dizzying leaps; in his studio attic on the Richelieu, Léon comes back on this day at the end of summer, to the Arcana of the Hermit, henceforth isolated on the table, and suddenly says, between two silences: "He knows, he dares, he is silent."

This "becoming oneself" seems to me to form the very fabric of the search of Léon Bellefleur, in the continuity of his work and under the illumination of the Ninth Arcana of Tarot; and this quest finds its force of attraction in its coded, mythical, inaccessible and absolute dimension, according to which Léon the Hermit continues his Work.

Surrealism and Childhood

With Bellefleur, the esoteric is neither an obsession nor a whim; he roots himself, on the contrary, in fundamental values, among which he finds favoured ones, Surrealism and Childhood; these values have been inseparably linked in the artist's imagination from the beginning of the forties, a period when they were important as well for Borduas and some other Montreal painters; with Bellefleur, these years were marked by many meetings with Pellan, who interpreted surrealism according to his own genius.

In 1946 Bellefleur presented his first exhibition along with works by his own children, and in the next year he published, in Les Ateliers d'Arts Graphiques, his "Plaidoyer pour l'enfant", in which he stated that "a child is almost always an artist and a poet"; this short article treats of the "way of mystery and the infinite", of the unspoiled, of spontaneity and of "genius" that is natural but so vulnerable and fragile, that a Paul Klee was often able to tame, that Miró and Kandinsky[3] worked hard to find sometimes — but that all academic education inevitably assassinates; Bellefleur knew whereof he spoke, since he would teach children the rudiments of knowledge for a quarter of a century from 1930 to 1954 and, even if this work as a teacher prevented him from devoting himself completely to his art, it no less remains that the magic presence of childhood was established in first place in his mind and sensitivity because, he would say, childhood is a privileged condition of discovery and wonder, of

play and dreams, to such a level of marvellous clairvoyance that "true maturity is that of the man who has kept intact his gifts as a child, who has developed them and who has dropped everything that had no relation to his nature"[4].

For what especially fascinated Léon Bellefleur in Surrealism was its sacred perspective, its magic illumination, its symbolical depth, its rituals and its analogies; what Surrealism offered him was a reading, an open interpretation of the universe and of the vast domain of art, where the occult dimensions of Dante or Bosch, of Blake or Rimbaud, of Cheval the postman or Ernst bloomed, according to an expansion of the imaginary impelling intuition and instinct to freely transmit the unforeseeable messages of the unconscious.

Bellefleur was not satisfied, however, to know Surrealism through the often opaque veil of books and periodicals; he regularly visited the Parisian surrealist group, chiefly from 1954 to 1966, and became friends with Breton, whom he was even able to accompany with a few close friends to Saint-Cirq-Lapopie; but much before the exciting encounters with Breton, Bellefleur had experienced the revelation of Surrealism in Montreal, as it had been explored by Pellan and then by Borduas; during the course of the forties, he had drawn "exquisite corpses" at Cap-à-l'Aigle with Mimi Parent and Jean Benoît (who themselves later became intimate with Breton), and he had cleared his own plastic, graphic and chromatic syntax.

And in his work nothing is given, nor, what is more, imposed, but everything is offered and half-open; it is enough for the gaze to coincide, for the soul to harmonize, and the Hermit allows our desires to enter into the pleasure of an astonishing cinema according to Edgar Morin's illumination in his 1958 book titled Le Cinéma, ou L'Homme imaginaire; the work comes into play immediately behind the gaze that invites it, and the profound visionary work unfurls its unforeseeable rhythms until the words swing in the direction where cold reason has access no longer, where analogy holds superb sway over inspired delirium, where the "alchemy of the verb" shocks Rimbaud himself and tears the pen from his fingers.

Henceforth initiated into the inexhaustible world of interior echoes and cosmic interchanges, Léon the Hermit indefectibly pursued his Quest, along the unforeseeable thread of his intuition and the accidents of the course, always listening for signs engraved on the profile of the everyday, open to the subtle play of reminiscences; the sleepless enchantment which could not possibly be mobilized from day to day, naturally, but which frequently renews the joy of his epiphany through drawings, prints or pictures, — these books of spells in front of which the eye learns to shut, to better see their endless metamorphoses and transmutations.

1. This would evoke the "inner model" of which André Breton spoke at the beginning of Le Surréalisme et la peinture (1928). Paris, Gallimard, 1965, p. 4.

2. Ibidem, p. 11.

3. It is not by chance that these three painters are mentioned, since they nourished the first three years of painting of Bellefleur, attracted also by primitive art and popular naïve art at the same time as children's art and surrealist art: his spiritual and plastic family thus comes at the same time from a high, deep lineage.

4. Léon Bellefleur, Plaidoyer pour l'enfant, in Les Ateliers d'Arts Graphiques. Montreal, 1947.

23

LEON BELLEFLEUR   BIOGRAPHICAL NOTES

     Léon Bellefleur was born in Montreal on February 8, 1910. Having graduated from Normal School in 1929, he was engaged as a teacher by the Catholic School Commission of Montreal; at the same time, he took evening courses at the School of Fine Arts from 1929 to 1938. He was then interested in children's drawings, in surrealism and in graphic automatism. In 1942, he attended Alfred Pellan's studio and made many *exquisite corpses*. In 1948, with Archambault, Dumouchel, Pellan, De Tonnancour and several others, he signed the *Prisme d'Yeux* manifesto and exhibited with the group at 3430 Ontario St. in Montreal. In 1949 Bellefleur was much interested by the work of Kandinsky and that of Miró. The painter subscribed to the surrealist theory on *objective accidents* and embraced graphic automatism. 1949 was a particularly important year for this artist, who found his way with a picture titled *Poissons rouges aux seins bleus* (National Gallery of Canada). In 1954 he left for Paris, where he studied etching at Friedlaender's studio. With a grant from the Canada Arts Council, he pursued his work at l'Atelier Desjobert, Paris, in 1958-1959. A member of the Canadian Society of Graphic Art and of the Canadian Painters Group in 1955, then of the Montreal Association of Non-figurative Artists in 1956, Léon Bellefleur finally settled in Quebec in 1966. He has received many prizes, among which is the Paul-Émile Borduas Prize (Plastic Arts), 1977, awarded by the Quebec Ministry of Cultural Affairs. His works appear in important public and private collections in Canada and abroad.

SELECTED BIBLIOGRAPHY

1954   *15 dessins de Léon Bellefleur;* introduction by R. H. Hubbard. Erta, Montreal.

1958   Michel van Schendel, *Cinéma des désirs*, in *Vie des Arts*, Vol. III, No. 12, pp. 19-26.

1959   Robert Ayre, *Léon Bellefleur*, in *Canadian Art*, Vol. 16.

1968   *Léon Bellefleur.* Catalogue of the exhibition at The National Gallery of Canada, Ottawa;
        Introduction by Jean-René Ostiguy; Essays by Roland Giguère and Gilles Hénault.
        Bernard Dagenais, *L'Espace lyrique et abstrait de Léon Bellefleur*, in *Vie des Arts*, Vol. XIII,
        No. 52, pp. 12-17.

1976   Gilles Daigneault, *Une autre saison de Léon Bellefleur*, in *Vie des Arts*, Vol. XXI, No. 84, pp. 46-47.

BOISVERT

Bernard LÉVY

Saint Lawrence Boulevard south of Pine Avenue. In the heart of Montreal. A third floor at the end of a staircase as steep as a ladder. A little door. Gilles Boisvert welcomes me into an immense flat where no partitions block the view: his studio.

No disorder around us. Just a few objects are lying around on a wide plank placed on two trestles: the work-bench. On the slightly peeling wall, a set square and a paint-brush are hanging. And then, against the back wall there are, one against the other, carefully arranged and protected by plastic, the most recent canvases (large nudes bathing) beside framed drawings (back from a past exhibition).

"Well, here's my studio," Gilles Boisvert says, and he adds, "very hot in summer, freezing in winter." The artist is not rich. He does not live a bohemian life (there is no bohemian life any more) but, at least for the present, a life in which commissions, grants, revenue from works sold in Montreal galleries, are very important. Also important is Boisvert's social involvement.

Two chairs, a stool, a high table, a metal filing cabinet: here is a corner favourable to conversation. We sit down near the windows, large glass panes without curtains that go from one wall to the other and that are filled with the light of a bright morning. The sun dazzles and warms our talk.

Is it still possible to speak of involvement for an artist of to-day?

Involvement is a word that is too restricted and at the same time very vague. And yet, I declare myself involved. Politically and socially. Not in the narrow meaning of the term politics that takes in concepts like partisanship, dogmatism, etc. These notions do not have much connection with art. I am involved because, in my opinion, an artist can't do otherwise. He is born of a social group. He can't deny his adherence to a social group. By virtue of this, he expresses in his way, which is certainly very personal, the life of this group which is also a part of his own life. The involvement is therefore human, first of all.

But isn't this utopian?

Yes, it's utopian, but necessary. I can't disclaim a great involvement in the world around me, that is very close to me and for which I feel partly responsible. When I look at it I never see it as an ensemble completely outside of myself. It is not abstract, nor am I. But perhaps I see myself as a Don Quixote . . .

Can you give me a concrete example?

This view of things is expressed badly with words, and still worse since it is a matter of a view tinged with humour. And so, take, for example, my picture in which the flag of Canada is hung with the help of a clothespin. You might say to yourself, "After all, we also wash flags, and they have to be dried, don't they?" But if you want to read something further into this, you are free to do so . . .

Do you make a living from your painting?

It's hard work, and it's better to take it with a dose of humour if one wants to survive. It's not easy. It has happened to me in some years that I produced works, sold them and lived only on the return from these sales. But usually, like many artists, I need added money, such as scholarships and grants. Luckily, an important contract, the commission and production of a mural (I'm thinking of the one I put up at Radio-Canada

House) is enough not only to support me for a whole year, but also permits me to undertake personal work without any material worries.

The contract formula should perhaps be exploited in a systematic way.

Yes, and more artists should be aware of it and understand how useful it is to be in groups, to help each other and to equip themselves with practical services. This points to the necessity of the Society of Contemporary Professional Artists of Quebec. This, thanks to a large membership, would be a pressure group that would really be listened to. I certainly stress the practical and utilitarian function of the society, not its aesthetic one. All the importance of a group lies in the fact that artists can be protected much more effectively as an organized social group than each individual would be able to do this separately for himself.

You prefer to work alone.

That's true, for several reasons. No doubt it's due to my nature, my temperament. And besides, I have many times tried to work in a group. The attempt is not without serious problems of co-ordination that end by becoming exhausting. In this case, it's necessary not only to have control of all the plans for the project that is to be produced but also to respect the creativity and the work rhythm of each of the participants, while taking into account technical and financial limits and, finally, delays. This type of experience is very interesting, but it is no less trying. As for the results, they are very unpredictable . . . Perhaps you remember *Pfff . . . Paf,* a collective environment presented in 1970 at the Museum of Contemporary Art (a giant heart was supposed to beat to the rhythm of music created to be used as counterpoint to the heartbeats; the whole thing was also synchronized with slides). This was a real adventure! But, all in all, I find myself more authentic, that is, more faithful to myself, when working alone.

The experience you have just recalled was meant to bring you closer to the public or to bring close to the public a work that you organized. You happened to "miss your mark": how do you react in the face of this kind of failure?

I try, through what I do, to keep as close as possible to the concerns of the people around me. I do my best to reach the public with a language that is my own, which is generally expressed on a canvas or a sheet of paper. If anyone remains indifferent to my works or if anyone asks me what "it means", I am certainly unable to react with words; from which I conclude that contact has not been established. But fortunately failures are quickly over: I have so many ideas and projects to produce . . . When one of them does not come off, I drop it, that's all. And besides, I don't wait for the public's reactions, I have confidence in my own judgment.

Where do you get your subjects from?

I find most of my subjects in current affairs. That is, at the heart of a reality made up of events perceived and shared by everyone. There are daily, familiar, simple incidents where things are mixed with dreams. Other occurrences are spectacular: demonstrations, wars, etc. Observe that I condemn nothing. I record. I express plastically what I feel. Then I hope

that my gesture will be understood, approved and shared, without the necessity of adding written or verbal commentaries. You see how essential the public is. That having been said, when I begin to compose a drawing, an oil or an engraving, I don't wonder if what I create is going to please such or such a group of people or not.

How do you proceed?

My way of working is first related to a style of gestural creation. I react spontaneously under a graphic form (drawings) to facts that I have found and sometimes cut out of newspapers or when looking at television. For me it is a matter of points of departure, of purpose. Then I rid myself of everything according to a Zen technique, to free the forms and signs of my subconscious.

This is how you explain the presence of numbers or geometric forms.

Yes, but without forgetting objects: keys, screws, different tools, billard balls and even hearts, sexes, waves, etc. I am facing a completely blank sheet of paper. With pencil in hand, I let the gesture take over as much as possible. Forms and objects appear. Then I try to find the right rhythm that will allow me to arrange them. It certainly happens that I go deeply into a theme: see the series *Les Oiseaux.* But in fact I don't know why a key, birds or waves catch my interest. These images pop up under my pencil. Perhaps it's a matter of imagination. Once more I am having trouble in expressing this with words. I'll give you an example. If I'm in the water and I want to represent water, I will try to suggest, not a way of *seeing* water but rather a way of perceiving it *tangibly.* I can say as much of light: I invent it.

By "letting the gesture take over" don't you risk falling into a certain incoherence?

It happens. There are sketches that come to nothing. I destroy them, just as writers do away with rough drafts with which they are not satisfied. But, as a matter of fact, by letting the gesture take over I remain myself. My creations gain unity in this way.

On this subject, one might speak of a style that is your own.

It is a fact that I keep only the successful gesture. It is in this way that, while progressively fitting forms with each other, I free a sense, a meaning. I recognize that there are subjects that command my attention more than others: waves, for instance. I believe that they allow me to establish a harmony between everything I produce and, perhaps, an evolution.

You haven't spoken to me of the place eroticism occupies in your works.

That's because eroticism is so much present in my life that it shows through without difficulty in my drawings or my canvases. For me, eroticism is a source of inspiration equal to current affairs. Indeed, they overlap each other. They form the same fabric . . .

Would you say that your production is generally autobiographical?

Certainly, since one can't dissociate oneself from what one does, but I would say rather that I am a witness and that's probably why I hope so much to be understood.

GILLES BOISVERT   **BIOGRAPHICAL NOTES**

Gilles Boisvert was born in Montreal on February 16, 1940. He studied at the Montreal School of Fine Arts from 1958 to 1960 before taking courses in engraving and lithography with Albert Dumouchel from 1961 to 1964.

His career began at Atelier Libre, which is now Guilde Graphique. Solo exhibitions immediately followed: in 1964, at the Claude Haeffely Gallery, and in the next year at Galerie 60. In 1966 the Museum of Contemporary Art exhibited his work. He also participated in group exhibitions. One of his works was selected in the Provincial Competition (1969). Since that time, Gilles Boisvert has been identified chiefly by his talent as a draughtsman. Into his pictures he inserts photographs on the subject of current events and frequently cut from daily newspapers. He also adds numerals and letters in violent colours.

Between 1969 and 1972, Boisvert was associated with the Pop movement, whose influence he recognized with *Pfff . . . Paf* (an inflatable sculpture environment) at the Museum of Contemporary Art (1970) and *Pack-Sack* (1971-1972), which travelled to Lausanne, Basle, Paris, Toronto, Montreal, Winnipeg, Rouyn and Sherbrooke.

Co-founder of Media Gallery in 1970, he presented in 1972 an important exhibition of serigraphs and photographs titled *Les Oiseaux*. The *Dessins* exhibition presented at the Museum of Contemporary Art at the end of 1972 was a great event, greeted as an undeniable success.

From that time, Gilles Boisvert has carried on an international career, as witnessed in 1976 by his exhibition at Galerie Shandar in Paris titled *Accrochez vos drapeaux*, where we rediscover his realist-surrealist-hyperrealist verve. His recent works have been shown at the Curzi Gallery in Montreal.

SELECTED BIBLIOGRAPHY

1970 Alain Hogue, *Gilles Boisvert, un peintre influencé par les thèmes de l'actualité*, in Le Soleil, Quebec, January 17.
Normand Thériault, *A l'heure de la contestation/Gilles Boisvert* in Vie des Arts, Vol. XIV, No. 58, pp. 102-103.
Un cœur a des hauts et des bas, in La Presse, Montreal, May 16.

1974 *Gilles Boisvert-Dessins*. Preface by Alain Parent; introduction by Claude Péloquin. Museum of Contemporary Art, Montreal.
Gilles Toupin, *Bye, bye Gilles Boisvert et au revoir*, in La Presse, November 23.
Claude Gosselin, *Trois expositions à la Cité du Havre*, in Le Devoir, Montreal, November 23.

1976 Henri Barras, *L'Univers en trompe-cœur de Gilles Boisvert* in Le Jour, Montreal, April 16.
Gilles Daigneault, *Gilles Boisvert, Une célébration de la salle de bain*, in Vie des Arts, Vol. XXI, No. 84, p. 64.

GAGNON

Germain LEFEBVRE

Charles Gagnon is a painter, film maker, photographer, something of a poet or a philosopher and certainly a well-informed lover of music, I hasten to explain. His environment is varied, changeable and filled with contradictions, as it should be!

The cottage in which he lives in Notre Dame de Grace is modest and hospitable. It is painted in a neutral colour, eggshell white, and the furniture or the ornaments that create animation are simple, unobtrusive and functional. And yet, upon looking more closely, one discovers here and there groups of objects whose presence appears suddenly curious or unusual, such as a collection of miniature glass bottles of varied shapes placed on the floor beside the fireplace, or again the precolumbian figurines from Guerrero grouped on a piece of furniture in the corner of the room.

From this interior space that forms the artist's immediate environment there emanates an atmosphere of serenity conducive to reflection and meditation. Charles Gagnon owns that for a long time he has been interested in oriental thought and in Zen, in particular.

As soon as one leaves this house, as soon as the door opens, it is as if a spell were suddenly broken. A hundred fifty feet ahead rise immense panels that mark an important exit of the Décarie expressway. We make it out very near, in the gaping trench humming with the noise of thousands of horsepower that emit their thick clouds of pollution.

Several times a week Charles Gagnon suffers this cultural shock, because he must leave his home to get to his place of work. He spends three days a week in the federal capital, where he is a professor in the Department of Visual Arts at the University of Ottawa. Besides, he devotes a great deal of time to his creative work in his studio in Old Montreal and, if he still has a few free moments, he goes to his farm near Ayer's Cliff in the Eastern Townships, where he also has a studio and where he also works, naturally!

From Notre Dame de Grace to Ottawa and from Old Montreal to Ayer's Cliff, Gagnon's itinerary seems very crowded to us. In spite of everything, this rhythm is maintained with a fine regularity and everything is taken care of smoothly, thanks to the willing participation of all the members of the Gagnon family.

All these persons, besides, are very busy, each with his own affairs. Michiko, Charles' wife, sees to the administration and animation of her art gallery, where first class artists exhibit. The children, for their part, do not have too much time to attend to their personal and school-related activities. The girls, Monika and Erika, of very different temperaments, are devoted, the one to the joys of writing, music and dance, the other to the rugged pleasure of hikes among wild natural scenes. The son,

Eames, is a determined hockey player whose progress is attentively followed by Charles, his chief admirer.

Charles Gagnon is not a man for social gatherings and is happy to avoid vernissages and official ceremonies. One can hardly say, so much does he hold himself apart, that he is part of what is called the artistic milieu. However, he is well known, respected and admired everywhere.

From the very beginning of his artistic career, Gagnon has always made his own way. When, at the age of twenty-one, he left Montreal in 1955 to work in New York, he had been very briefly introduced to the life of an artist as it is lived here. What he knew of it was from the hours he spent talking with Jimmy Jones and watching him work in his studio on Stanley St. or sipping coffee near there at Carmen's with a small group chiefly animated by Vittorio's presence.

Gagnon never attended the École du Meuble, the School of Fine Arts or the School of Applied Arts, and Pellan or Borduas and the Automatists were for him, at that time, only names that he could without doubt relate to certain works seen in exhibitions, nothing more. When Molinari opened Galerie L'Actuelle which became an ardent artistic centre, Gagnon had already left for the American metropolis. It was only in 1958 that he made the acquaintance of the plasticians, Molinari and Tousignant, on the occasion of his first solo exhibition at Galerie Artek.

The departure for New York is in no way linked to a movement, a style or a tradition of stages of study or pilgrimages such as were still being carried on some decades earlier in the Québécois milieu, toward the great Paris schools. Certainly, there was Borduas who spent time in New York at that period and doubtless some others too, but in an unplanned and irregular fashion. The exhibition titled *Modern Canadian Painters* that Molinari organized in 1956 for New York's Parma Gallery, in spite of its interest, did not really inspire a concerted movement of Montreal artists to this city that was becoming the new world capital of art. Saxe, Hurtubise and Daglish came to stay there, but for a relatively short period.

If Gagnon settled in New York, it was in order to able to be closer to and participate in the great revolution in American art, this uprising of abstract expressionist painting which had been revealed to him by an article in *The Times* and which filled him with enthusiasm. He lived there almost five years and attended New York University as well as the New York School of Design.

However, it was by tirelessly visiting the avant-garde galleries that he deepened his artistic knowledge and that little by little he defined the bases of his aesthetic involvement. He went regularly to Sidney Jarvis, Martha Jackson, Betty Parson, Kootz Gallery, Stable Gallery and Green's. At that time one could quite easily approach painters who to-day are very great celebrities, and Gagnon remembers having timidly and briefly spoken with Robert Motherwell when the latter was lunching alone in a little restaurant. Sundays were reserved for the traditional pilgrimage to the Museum of Modern Art to admire chiefly the Monets and the Cézannes, and to the Metropolitan Museum of Art where he enjoyed seeing the Egyptian or Sumerian antiquities.

Upon his return to Montreal, Gagnon lost no time in joining the artistic circle, and in a few years he exhibited successively in the most active galleries, at Denyse Delrue's, Camille Hébert's and Agnès Lefort's. From the beginning, he got the warmest reception from the critics. Robert Ayre, Jacques Folch, Lawrence Sabbath and Claude Jasmin encouraged the first developments of his young career.

Gagnon soon appeared in the principal group exhibitions beside the best-known artists on the Canadian scene and in 1963 obtained a first solo exhibition at the Montreal Museum, in Norton gallery.

Then, as in a well-greased machine, events moved along in the smoothest harmony, so that to-day, at the beginning of his forties, Charles Gagnon has climbed all the rungs of the ladder to success: he has represented Canada in numerous international exhibitions; the Canada Council has granted him its support; the creations he produced for the Agriculture, the Christian and the Hydro-Quebec Pavilions at the Montreal Universal Exposition of 1967 have given him an international reputation; his pictures, drawings or photographs appear in the most important collections of the country.

Briefly, here is an accomplished *pro,* and if the star system were to reach, in the domain of the visual arts, the heights to which it has arrived in the theatrical arts, there is no doubt that Gagnon would have to yield to autograph-seekers. God knows, however, how jealously he guards his privacy and does his best to keep the most direct contact with the most commonplace everyday events, and the most nearly anonymous. "I have abandoned intellectualism to uncover flesh and blood men, who go on picnics, eat hot dogs, chew gum and go to the barber," he said to Claude Jasmin in 1962[1]. He has not changed his attitude since then.

Certainly, his environment bears the indelible marks of the presence everywhere of the artistic fact. Gagnon has many acquaintances and friends in the arts milieu, among whom are his professor colleagues, for the most part transplanted from Montreal to Ottawa and with whom he has the opportunity of conversing. Then again, until very recently, painters Yves Gaucher and Jean McEwen had their studios in the same building as he did, and he saw them with pleasure. His unfinished film, which he called *R-69,* also formed, originally, a report on the creation of an immense red picture by Gaucher and later became a personal testimony on the art world in Montreal.

Gagnon does not tend to discuss his paintings with a formalist view, without, however, denying the interest of this kind of exercise. Particularly, he does not display the dogmatic attitude of the theoretician, and his comments lead us to think much more of the evocations of the symbolist poets who were interested in the connections between the many perceptions of the senses and, from there, between the different forms of art. Gagnon feels the need to use freely varied forms of expression like photography, film or painting, because he believes that the media are only tools in the service of the artist, who can bend them to the demands of the project on hand. This is certainly not a common attitude in the Montreal artistic climate, an attitude that Gagnon has adopted from his New York stay and that is the result of his experience with happenings, multi-disciplinary events instigated by the group of John Cage, Merce Cunningham and Robert Rauschenberg, among others. It is a form of liberation from the framework of creation, of expression, an expansion of the environment at the very level of its psychic and spiritual dimensions.

Charles Gagnon frequently alludes to a religious or spiritual dimension when he discusses his art, and it certainly seems that it is this reality that weaves the fabric where the varied aspects of his work are joined.

Music plays an important rôle in his work — it was he who conceived the sound tracks of his film productions. He bathes almost constantly in a musical atmosphere, since he has a stereo everywhere he stays regularly. His taste is rather conservative, as he says. He collects Bach and particularly Mozart and, naturally, all the jazz greats with a special passion that causes him sometimes to obtain a large choice of the most important recordings of the same selection. He owns Bach's *Well-Tempered Clavier* in seven versions.

In photography and cinema, it is the immediate reality that serves as primary material in the production of every work and, in this regard, real environment becomes highly significant.

On examining photographs Gagnon has exhibited until now, one would never guess the existence, somewhere in Charles Gagnon's everyday life, of a farm surrounded by hills, brooks and prairies. But the absurdity of our urban landscape, its brutality and its chaos in the noisy and malodorous concrete jungle style, burst forth in many variations. There are blind concrete facades, abandoned parking lots, deserted parts of streets, long lines of bare office buildings or small islands of greenery isolated in a sea of asphalt; all places from which the human presence seems to have departed for good. By means of a restrained, even simplified language, Gagnon expresses an implacable commentary on the socio-cultural disasters whose present extensions still hardly succeed to-day in troubling or affecting the planners of our urban habitat.

Beyond differences of vocabulary, this photographic expression presents profound affinities with Gagnon's pictorial aesthetics, even when the latter appears in a most abstract form, as his friend, the theoretician and art critic Philip Fry, has shown. In the ensemble of his work, Charles Gagnon tends to establish very close contact with the spectator, and as Fry emphasizes, "Gagnon's work produced in the studio leads to communion rather than to communication because it offers the form of the contents and invites the spectator to bring to it the substance arising from his person."[2]

For the moment, Charles Gagnon is preparing to push this communion still further by unveiling in a coming exhibition certain results of *archaelogical* digs that he undertook on some little-known sectors of his old works and by giving out at the same time the results of his most recent prospecting.

1. Claude Jasmin, *Gagnon* in *Canadian Art,* March-April 1962.
2. Philip Fry, *Charles Gagnon: faire et prendre* in *Parachute* 8, Autumn 1977.

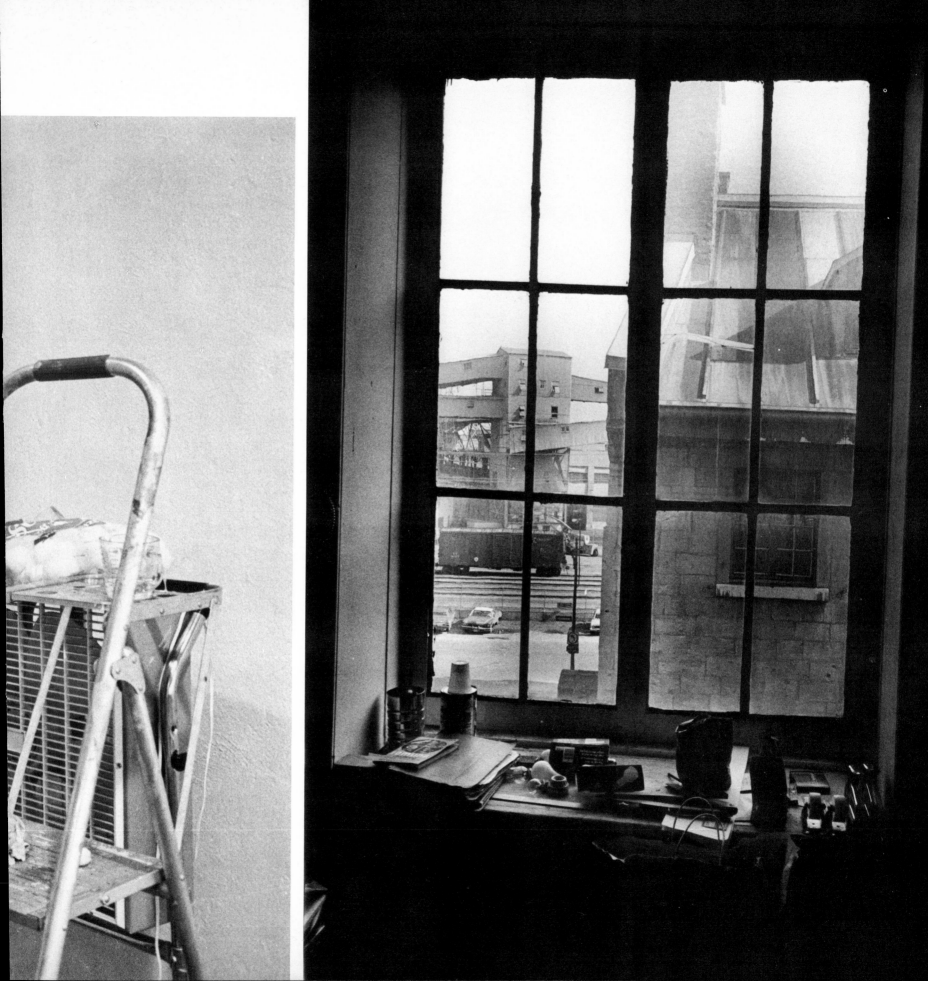

CHARLES GAGNON   BIOGRAPHICAL NOTES

A painter, cineast and photographer, Charles Gagnon was born in Montreal in 1934. He studied for a short time at Montreal before entering the interior decorating course at the Parsons School in New York in 1956. Later, he studied painting at the Art Students League as well as at New York University. He returned to Montreal in 1960, and received a grant from the Canada Arts Council in 1961 and 1968. He won an honourable mention at the Spring Exhibition of the Montreal Museum of Fine Arts in 1963 and 1965. Charles Gagnon is presently a professor in the Visual Arts Faculty of the University of Ottawa.

SELECTED BIBLIOGRAPHY

1958   Rodolphe de Repentigny, in *La Presse*, Montreal, October 15.

1961   Claude Jasmin, *Charles Gagnon ou l'éclatement des cadres*, in *La Presse*, October 7.
        Jacques Folch-Ribas, *Charles Gagnon*, in *Vie des Arts*, Vol. VI, No. 25, p. 53.

1962   Claude Jasmin, *Charles Gagnon*, in *Canadian Art*, No. 78.
        Laurent Lamy, *Charles Gagnon et John Fox au Musée*, in *Le Devoir*, Montreal, November 8.

1963   *Arte de America y Espana*, in *Blanco y Negro*, Madrid, June 22.

1964   Laurent Lamy, *Charles Gagnon à la Galerie Camille Hébert*, in *Le Devoir*, January 25.
        Claude Jasmin, *Charles Gagnon — Cerner le réel*, in *La Presse*, January 25.

1966   Yves Robillard, *Charles Gagnon: Une entrée dans un tableau*, in *La Presse*, October 29.
        Robert Ayre, *The Works of Charles Gagnon*, in *The Montreal Star*, October 29.

1967   H. M. Kinzer, *Expography* in *Popular Photography*, October.

1968   *Canadian Art* in *The Scotsman*, Edinburgh, August 21.
        Normand Thériault, *Charles Gagnon*, in *Vie des Arts*, Vol. XIII, No. 53, pp. 28-33.

1969   Normand Thériault, *Lithographs by Takao Tanabe and Charles Gagnon* in *Artscanada*, Toronto, February.
        Normand Thériault, *Le Tableau est aussi le monde* in *La Presse*, March 8, p. 34.
        Robert Ayre, *Stability in a Changing World*, in *The Montreal Star*, March 15.
        B. Lord, *New Work from Montreal, Gagnon, Ewen, Molinari*, in *Art in America* (USA), May-June.

1970   D. Corbeil, *Charles Gagnon, Artist, Filmaker lives in Montreal*, in *Artscanada*, April.
        A. Lerner, *A Window on Canadian Art*, in *Davar*, Israel, November 20.
        R. Bermar, *More Than Meets the Eye*, in *Jerusalem Post Magazine*, November 27.

1972   Catherine Bates, *Comic Books and Real Life*, in *The Montreal Star*, November 18.

1974   *Charles Gagnon — Témoignage*, in *Ovo/Photo*, Montreal, June.
        Robert Marteau, *L'Art et la manière* in *Le Jour*, Montreal, June 1.
        Henry Lehmann, *Powerful Restraint*, in *The Montreal Star*, June 1, p. D-9.
        Gilles Toupin, *Charles Gagnon: Le Combat des fous vers l'infini*, in *La Presse*, June 8, p. E16.
        Hugo McPherson, *The Compleat Artist*, in *Artscanada*, No. 31, pp. 79-81.
        Gilles Toupin, *La Nudité du paysage urbain*, in *La Presse*, January 24, p. D20.
        Henry Lehmann, *Reality Intrudes*, in *The Montreal Star*, January 31, p. D-4.

1976   Gilles Toupin, *Une photographie en train de s'affirmer*, in *La Presse*, July 31.
        P. Cousineau, *Two Photographic Exhibitions*, in *Parachute*, No. 4, pp. 6-9.

1977   P. Richard, *Choice Canadian Color*, in *The Washington Post*, February 3.
        Philip Fry, *Charles Gagnon: Making and Taking*, in *Parachute*, No. 8, pp. 8-13.

GAUCHER

François-Marc GAGNON

At the exhibition that he had titled *Perspective*[1], Yves Gaucher, making himself his own critic, had not chosen to present to us a retrospective of his work but instead to open for us a *perspective* on it, allowing him as well as us to emphasize one of his essential courses. The exhibition closed on an immense, particularly imposing and astonishing picture (it measured 9½ by 16 feet). Wedged between two horizontal bands, the one at the top wider than the one at the bottom, two expanses separated by a diagonal occupied almost the whole field of the picture. These two areas formed so many cut up triangles of uneven surface, the larger being reversed and pressing on the hypotenuse of the other. Thus there was a certain correspondence between the surface of the horizontal bands and that of the triangles. On the other hand, the most striking aspect, besides the extremely dark colouring of the picture, its "grays" being almost black, arose from the tensions introduced into the picture between the central area and the periphery on the one hand, and the left and right fields of the central area, on the other. All this occurred as if the central area, under the pressure of a turn of the screw from top and bottom at the same time and therefore vertically, had had no other choice but to slide laterally, thus creating a gigantic break, the famous diagonal crossing the central area from the right above, and toward the left at the bottom. For those among us who associate Gaucher with the gray pictures in the Godard Lefort 1969 exhibition or even the 1963 engraving series, *En hommage à Webern,* it was a real surprise! Instead of the extremely pale gray field slightly tinted with pink, green, blue or violet, we were faced with *two browns* and *two grays* almost black, very powerful and enforced. Instead of off-centre signals floating on the surface of the field, we saw the large diagonal. Much more, the exhibition revealed a whole dimension of Gaucher's work that we had not seen in Montreal or about which we knew very little. The last flash on Gaucher's recent development, if my memory serves me well, was a red monochromatic picture painted with fluorescent paint and crossed by a thin white opening which even included red smudges. In his article, *Synthèse de perspective, 1976*[2], Gaucher had pointed out that with his picture, *R-69*, he had introduced a "total break" in his work, followed in 1970 by a period of "groping". Obviously it was a matter of a picture by which the painter intended to escape his own limits and the *image* of his gray paintings that had been comfortable for critics and the public. But on what had followed this antithetical picture we were in the dark.

Champ vert, a 1971 painting, indicates, however, the new direction taken since then by Gaucher. Four lines divide the area horizontally in five bands of uneven surface. The lines cross the whole pictorial plane and constitute only interruptions in the *green field*. Of uneven surface, the horizontal bands command attention as the picture's prime element and introduce the principle of an asymmetrical arrangement of the elements in the picture, otherwise than by oppositions of vertical or horizontal lines or black or gray squares.

Later, even the lines of division between the bands were eliminated, as in *Brun, jaune, rouge* of 1973. The intervention of the lines was no longer considered necessary, since the clear demarcation of one field of colour against the other could play that rôle. While the lines in *Champ vert* introduced the idea of an interruption of the field, in *Brun, jaune, rouge* the colour by itself produced this effect. When, a little later, the bands had the same thickness, as in 1974's *Vert, brun, bleu et ocre*, the variations of tint, tonality and saturation in each band would maintain the principle of asymmetry.

In the commentaries recorded on video with which Gaucher accompanied his exhibition, he next noted that "from 1973 to 1976 each series of pictures points directly toward research in the essential base of [his] work: the diagonal". He could therefore state that *Deux bruns, deux gris*, the most recent picture in the exhibition, did not mark a break with "the complex cycle begun in '69 (or in '63), but was its outcome, while announcing a new *problem*: that of the *diagonal*. Certainly, in the *perspective* Gaucher thus applied to his work, he was obliged to subtract many of the aspects often noted concerning his pictures and to which he had himself called attention in his 1976 article: the "non-physicality" of the work, its unsubstantial character, since the "experiment" with "colour" is implicit in it; the importance of the concept of "duration" in the perception of the work; the "subliminal experience" that the viewer feels of some elements of the picture that enters his perceptual field even before he has paid attention to them; the compulsory "creative participation" of the "viewer" to introduce the "duration" element into the picture and make it work . . . Inevitably, attention was brought back now upon the structure underlying the whole work, which Gaucher defined as the progressive passing of a rhythm symmetrical to an asymmetrical language and with asymmetry as the more and more imperative affirmation of the diagonal. We were invited at the same time to re-read Gaucher's work, from *En hommage à Webern* to the present. The importance of the 1963 engravings, which are in reality "impressions in relief on laminated paper" and which had been inspired by hearing a concert by Webern in Paris at the beginning of 1962, was reaffirmed. Not only was the reduction of elements to vertical and horizontal bars, to black or gray squares, to hollows or to reliefs significant, but their chance arrangement "founded on a certain triangulation", as Bernard Teyssèdre remarked at the time, was no less significant. Even if, in a recent interview (October 1976) with Normand Thériault, Gaucher displayed some irritation in connection with the close similarities that continue to be perceived between music and his works, it still remains that not only did he take the trouble to verify the limits of this connection himself in autumn 1968 at the laboratory of electronic music at McGill University, but that he also had recourse several times to titles evoking selections of oriental music (*Raga, Alap*), popular (square dances) or contemporary music (*Homage to Berlioz, Point/Counterpoint, Pli selon pli*, this last title borrowed outright from Boulez). Besides, the including of the duration factor would by itself alone be enough to give weight to the rapprochement with music. In my opinion, it does not seem superficial to bring the engravings, *En hommage à Webern*, close to the music, made of silence and brief, sonorous intervals, avoiding repetitions and rhythmic redundancies to rely on a random construction. Gaucher's subsequent work showed the structural character of this factor in his development. When, a little earlier in 1961 he had become interested in "Hindu philosophy" and had discovered an interest in Indian music, especially that of Ali Akbar Khan, virtuoso on the *sarod* (less a *star* than his brother-in-law, Ravi Shankar), he showed a great coherence in his inclinations. In the *raga,* the monotone background played on the *tanpura* could correspond to Webern's silences, and the development of the piece that takes place in three stages, the *alap,* the *jor* and the *jhala,* in a faster and faster tempo already announced a style of composition in which the crossing of a big diagonal was structural. Moreover, Hindu music, always giving the most important part to improvisation, made place for the problematical, to which our music (except jazz and a part of contemporary experimental music) is, in general, a total stranger. Finally, *raga* at its highest point often integrated the figure of the *sawal-jawab* (question and answer), the melodic instrument announcing a figure that the *tabla* then reproduced rhythmically, thus creating a real dialogue, the nearest equivalent to spoken exchange that can be conceived in music. The asymmetry is extreme, since one of the existing poles is melodic, the other rhythmic. If he lent an attentive ear at the time of his sojourn in Egypt to the chant of the muezzin reciting verses of the Koran from the balcony of the mosque or from the top of the minaret, Gaucher has been able to test a perhaps still more advanced form of symbiosis between language, music and silence. The interruptions and the gaps with which the cantor punctuates his recitation catch up with Webern's *silences* or the *tanpura*'s murmur but the melody, in the interval, is a holy phrase that serves as support for meditation.

Gaucher then called attention to the suite of lithographs titled *Transitions* that immediately preceded his gray pictures. His previous propositions underwent a further simplification. The square, the surface, the very opposition of the vertical and horizontal lines creating balances of forces in Mondrian fashion were omitted. The work was reduced now to some horizontal lines of different lengths and extremely unobtrusive intensities, but which polarized the field, defining in it regions of unequal expanse and presence. The vertical was kept only by implication since on their departure or arrival the horizontal lines were joined in columns or in bundles.

In the gray pictures produced next, from December 1967 to October 1969, the principles at work in the lithographs of the series *Transitions* were applied and carried to their greatest power. The gray pictures marked a summit in Gaucher's work. I remember that what struck me most at the time of their presentation at Godard Lefort's in 1969 was the integration of duration into the painting. It was impossible to wholly understand the picture, if not as a lightly tinted gray field. As soon as one directed his attention to the signals, that is the light white or gray lines, the picture became animated, revealing an event in a corner, then another some time later in the opposite corner. The very expanse of the support's surface prevented one's being able to perceive with one glance the ensemble of the events occupying the pictorial area. The music seemed to have found its exact pictorial equivalent, but it was a matter of an arhythmic music, risky, that the viewer had time to arrange and rearrange in as many ways as he pleased. It is not surprising that these pictures made a great impression at Edinburgh and at London when some of them were shown there in 1968. The English critic, Bryan Robertson, described them magnificently and drew attention to the musical effect of the coloured lines in the gray field. "They set up a dialogue with each other and very quickly become as concentrated and meaningful as the sound bleeps on some slowly moving tape of new music, made with totally unfamiliar means." Also, the pictures exhibited at Edinburgh were titled *Alap,* from the term that is used to designate the slow, arhythmic and improvised movement of the *ragas* and which precedes the part where the intervening *tabla,* rhythm and acceleration take possession of the piece.

At the end of 1969, as we have seen, Gaucher felt the need to escape the trap that for him was the summit already reached and questioned his success. We had to wait for *Champ vert* the following year to see him take off toward another peak, of which *Deux bruns, deux gris* marks the result.

Gaucher's fascination with asymmetry, for the diagonal, gives him a place quite apart in the development of contemporary minimal art. We know that the diagonal haunted Mondrian, who saw in it the door open to the expression of the hated "tragic" and therefore of "naturalism". Albers, in his *Homages to the Square,* meditated endlessly on the symmetrical figure par excellence, the square. Even Frank Stella's black pictures developed from symmetrical motifs. It is Gaucher's strength to be able to approach the *dangerous* zones of asymmetry without falling into abstract landscapism, because with him asymmetry is not the fruit of a sort of stylization of the real but the structural principle of the work.

---

1. Presented at the Museum of Contemporary Art, from October 7 to November 7, 1976.

2. Reproduced by Normand Thériault in issue No. 6 of *Parachute* magazine.

Pages
49 The artist in his studio on St. Paul St.
50, 51, 52, 54 and 55 The artist in his new studio.
53 *2 bleus-2 gris*, 1976.
Acrylic on canvas; 287 x 485,6 cm.
54 The house, . . . a taste for collections.
Photographic report by Sam Tata.

YVES GAUCHER BIOGRAPHICAL NOTES

Born in Montreal in 1934, Yves Gaucher studied at the Fine Arts School from 1954 to 1956. In 1959 he received first prize for engraving at the Montreal Young Painting Exhibition. In 1961 he won first prize in the Quebec Artistic Competition (which he would obtain a second time in 1963) as well as the one in the Burnaby National Engraving Competition. Interested in music and particularly by composer Anton von Webern, in 1963 he began a series of engravings titled *En hommage à Webern*. He has participated in many international exhibitions.

His works are exhibited in Canada as well as in the United States, in England, in South Africa and in Yugoslavia. At present, Yves Gaucher is a professor at Concordia University.

SELECTED BIBLIOGRAPHY

1962 Paul Martin-Dubost, *Les Cuivres martelés d'Yves Gaucher*, in *Le Nouveau Journal*, Montreal, November 25.

1963 Ruth Auesperg, *Yves Gaucher at Galerie Agnès Lefort*, in *Canadian Art Magazine*, Vol. 20.

1965 Jacques Folch-Ribas, *Yves Gaucher*, in *Vie des Arts*, Vol. X, No. 41, pp. 40-43.

1967 Manon Gaulin, *Toward Serenity*, in *Time Magazine* (Canadian edition), May 26.

1968 Anne Brodzky, *Notice Also Silence Sounds*, in *Artscanada*, June, pp. 21-23.

1969 Normand Thériault, *Prélude à une exposition*, in *La Presse*, Montreal, February 4.
Yves Gaucher. Introduction by Doris Shadbolt, Vancouver Art Gallery.
Robert Millet, *Gaucher: Manipuler l'œil*, in *Chatelaine*, October.
Marie Raymond, *Yves Gaucher à Londres*, in *Vie des Arts*, Vol. XIV, No. 57, p. 56.
John Noel Chandler, *Dialogue at an Exhibition of Yves Gaucher's Grey Paintings*, in *Artscanada*, No. 26, pp. 3-6.
David P. Silcox, *Yves Gaucher*, in *Studio International*, No. 177, February, pp. 76-77.

1972 Michael White, *The Quiet Voice of Yves Gaucher*, in *The Montreal Gazette*, January 22.

1973 Michel Ragon, *Yves Gaucher, Rêverie de l'absolu*, in *Vie des Arts*, Vol. XVII, No. 70, pp. 28-33.
William James Gordon Kirby, *A Discussion of Five Canadian Painters — Ronald Bloore, Brian Fisher, Yves Gaucher, Roy Kiyooka, Arthur McKay, — in the Context of the Artistic and Critical Sensibility of the 1960's*. Master's thesis at the University of British Columbia.

1975 Geoffrey James, *Yves Gaucher's Silent Sounds*, in *Time Magazine* (Canadian edition), March 24.
Gaucher, New York Cultural Center, 24 pages.
Dore Ashton, *Gaucher at New York Cultural Center*, in *Artscanada*, June.

1976 Georges Bogardi, *Yves Gaucher*, in *The Montreal Star*, October 16, p. D-5.
Gilles Toupin, *Un plongeon dans la couleur*, in *La Presse*, October 23, p. C26.
Perspective 1963-1976: Yves Gaucher, peintures et gravures. Introduction by Alain Parent; Articles by various critics. Museum of Contemporary Art, Montreal.

1977 Bernard Tesseydre, *Coloris et structure chez un peintre contemporain de Montréal, Yves Gaucher*, in *Ateliers*, Vol. 5, No. 3.
Normand Thériault, *Yves Gaucher: The Last Picture Shown*, in *Parachute*, No. 6, pp. 38-41.

GOULET

Gilles RIOUX

The arrow of Zeno of Elea does not fly. In a paradox of another kind, but no less fascinating, Claude Goulet's pictures do not move.

Whether the support was of an exterior and objective subject or of an interior and subjective representation, the picture began to overcome its status as an autonomous object only a century ago, when the Impressionists placed a screen of material between their painted subjects and the viewer. Until that time, paint was just a cheap material out of a tube, placed on the palette and which the artist knew how to hide cleverly, by means of little brush strokes blending with each other in an image. With the Impressionists, paint as material came into its own for the first time, made itself dazzling and spread itself shamelessly in large sweeps on the surface of the canvas. The people of that time understood this well and were indignant at this gritty surface catching the eye and upsetting their mental vision of the subject. Thanks to this break-through, in 1890 a young man of twenty, Maurice Denis, drew up in direct terms this genuine postulate of all modern painting: "One must remember that a picture — before being a charger, a naked woman or some anecdote or other — is essentially a plane surface covered with colours assembled in a certain order".[1]

Later, others would come to widen this breach: Picasso and Braque with their glued papers, the Dadaists with their collages and insertion of different objects, the Expressionists with their vehement colours, Matisse with his flat tints. All of them asserted themselves, and, each in his way, pointed out the materiality of the picture. Doubtless it is possible to state cautiously that the picture became more materialistic — in the etymological sense of the term. Simultaneously, the picture was emptied of its exterior subject and became its own subject; it no longer tended to substitute itself for any exterior reality, but definitely to become its own object, its own finality. This evolution is seen as much in non-figurative lyrical works as in geometric abstract pictures. And in this connection it is not unimportant to notice that the trajectory of Claude Goulet's work is parallel to that traced by the passage to Montreal Automatism in the Plasticians' activity. With most kinetic artists, he shares the fact of having first received a scientific education (he is a biochemist), which is strongly likely to determine a much more methodical approach to pictorial activity denuded of the emotional trash with which it too often uselessly adorns itself.

These rapid reflections are not so much a historical recall and the statement of a few facts as a display of them, made necessary on account of the points of contact with Goulet's work that they offer. A fundamental attitude in which he believes unshakeably; Goulet considers the production of works of art as a specialized activity that should be entrusted to technicians who have received appropriate training. More and more technical, more and more material in its development, the work of art is little by little losing its supposedly magic contents and, with it, the status of the artist is also modified; the time is not far off when it will be neither more prestigious nor more shameful to call one-self an artist than to identify oneself as an electronics specialist, a doctor or an economist. Besides, the moment has arrived when artists have abandoned the beret, the flowing tie and the smock and that only a part of the public regrets these things, not so much as necessary accessories of the profession but rather as attributes still loaded with symbolical significance and fit to support the imagination.

In this tortuous road of subjectivity, the very road of Lyrical Abstraction, Action Painting and Abstract Expressionism, Claude Goulet insists on emphasizing that in spite of appearances the lyrical contents of his pictures in the first manner should be put between brackets, because he conceived them with a sharp sense of matter, texture and relief. In brief, they are first of all tactile objects. An adjustment of this nature bears a very special importance since it clearly indicates that the advent of a geometrically constructed art does not constitute a break with the past, but the passing from a rather informal stage to a more formalist stage, recent works being virtually contained in the earlier ones. Change is registered in the organization of material on the surface, organization which is carried on henceforth in a more rigid form.

Goulet's art passes first through the perfecting of a thoroughly simple, subtle and effective technique. Essentially, it consists of throwing on the canvas a layer of sand mixed with a binder; this results in a granular surface formed of innumerable little asperities hardly a few millimetres high. Colour is applied with a spray gun and the subtlety consists of pulverizing it at a very acute angle, skimming the surface of the picture, so that only half of these rough places is painted; then the other face is painted, still in the same manner but with a different colour from the first one. In this way, each sandy point is coloured in one colour on the right and in another on the left. In spite of the differences in the method of applying the colour, one cannot miss calling to mind the vibrant texture of the surface of impressionist canvases and the light shimmer that runs over them. To this pointillist technique — the term will be allowed us — corresponds a divisionism of the blob of pigment on one or other of the two faces of the little bumps and their optical mixture when we observe them from a distance. Goulet shares with the Impressionists and the Neo-impressionists a similar taste for the intense chromatism of the colours used and the optic fusion of these colours in softer and more blurred values. And, in the manner of many impressionist pictures, the surface is never totally static, as it seems incessantly animated by a tiny shimmering.

Goulet's technique, thanks to granular surface's relief, permits rather astonishing effects of permutation. Imagine a square picture whose points are blue on the right and red on the left; the front view of the picture will operate the optical blending of these two colours and the spectator will see a violet square; let the viewer move along the wall and look at the same picture from the side: on the right he will see an all-blue picture and on the left an all-red one. This very simple experiment with a plane surface illustrates very well the possibilities contained in this technique if varied structures are introduced. Historically, it was El Lissitzky who first explored these possibilities in 1926-1927 in his *Galerie abstraite* on whose walls were hung thin bands of metal painted white on one side, black on the other. As he moved about the room, the viewer saw the wall pass gradually from black to white after going through all the shades of gray. In our day, Yaacov Agam uses a procedure very close to this, where this time the support is made up of angles whose left faces are painted to produce a motif when they are seen in succession, while the right faces present a different motif and the frontal view merges the two. Much credit is certainly due Claude Goulet for having known how to reduce the relief of the surface to a minimal elevation and for having been able to obtain no less clear results.

Simple in its basic elements, Claude Goulet's technique gains in subtleness through the organization of pictorial space into zones at first slightly complex and to-day much more inextricable. Eight or ten years ago, parallel bands crossed by a circle, a symmetrical motif, or else two or three concentric geometrical forms constituted, on the whole, the main feature of the picture's structure. Each of these forms being painted on two facets, in the way we have spoken of, we then witness a threefold multiplication of the pictorial space. The paradox of this space results from the fact that in the stable and rigid framework of the structure, inherent in the picture's bidimensional reality, we can see three formally similar pictures, but of different colours. All this takes place as if on a single surface were painted three distinct — and superimposed — pictures.

This triple perception in the uniquity of a single picture causes movement to take place — the movement of the spectator called upon to move laterally in front of the work in such a way as to follow the transformation of the coloured fields to their maximum of saturation. Therefore there exist three favoured points of view, corresponding to the *three* pictures: at the left, at the centre and at the right; but between these three points there is a multitude of intermediary positions which have to be crossed slowly in order to perceive the change that is taking place on the canvas. In the end positions, on the right and on the left, we observe that a *positive* configuration on one side becomes *negative* on the other. In fact, this reversal rests on the systematic utilization of opposition between light and dark values. Thus it would probably be more suitable to say that the images of the left and the right are antithetical.

Less evident but no less present and acting in the perception of the picture, the time factor is closely linked to the movement. Certainly this is a matter, on the one hand, of the precise time necessary to move from one side of the work to the other; but on the other hand it involves above all the psychological time invested in the exploration of the picture. A notion of time also eminently subjective, called upon to expand or contract according to the moment and the nature of the visual experience.

In Claude Goulet we have, without knowing it, a major figure in kinetic art. More and better than all we could say or write, the constancy of his development and his persistance at work are still the best guarantees of his being recognized.

---

1. *Théories*, Paris, 1920, p. 1.

CLAUDE GOULET   BIOGRAPHICAL NOTES

Claude Goulet was born in Montreal on June 5, 1925. A graduate of the Faculty of Chemistry at the University of Montreal, he took his artistic studies at the Montreal School of Fine Arts. In 1967 he was named secretary of the Contemporary Society of Professional Artists of Quebec, then vice-president in 1968-1969. He has participated in several exhibitions across Quebec, Canada, the United States, Europe and Japan. A member of the Royal Canadian Academy as well as of the Canadian Conference of the Arts, Claude Goulet teaches at the Arts Faculty of the University of Quebec at Three Rivers.

SELECTED BIBLIOGRAPHY

1967   Charlemagne Bouchard, *Goulet, le peintre des couleurs qui bougent*, in *La Patrie*, Montreal, February 12.
        Virginia Lambe, *A Careful Colour Really Changes*, in *The Montreal Gazette*, November 25.
        Master of Change, in *Time Magazine* (Canadian edition), November 24, pp. 24-25.
        Yves Robillard, *Des tableaux qui changent avec le jour*, in *La Presse*, Montreal, November 25, p. 34.

1969   *La Couleur crée le mouvement*, in *La Presse*, November 29.
        Michael White, *Optical Works that Move*, in *The Montreal Star*, May 17.
        Grazia Merler, *Le Multidimensionnel: mutations des lignes et de la lumière*, in *Le Soleil*, Quebec.

1970   Paul Dumas, *Claude Goulet, poète des métamorphoses*, in *L'Information médicale et paramédicale*, February 17, p. 16.
        Normand Thériault, *Le Tableau mur à mur*, in *La Presse*, January 31.

1971   Luc Benoit, *Claude Goulet*, in *Vie des Arts*, Vol. XVI, No. 63, pp. 66-67.
        Claude Goulet — Multidimensionnels, Canadian Cultural Centre, Paris. 24 pages.

1977   François-Marc Gagnon, *Claude Goulet, peintre géomètre*, in *Vie des Arts*, Vol. XXI, No. 86, pp. 46-47.

HURTUBISE

André PARINAUD

After Borduas (pioneer of Tachism and Lyrical Abstraction), after Riopelle, Canada has just discovered a great painter's temperament — a natural — in Jacques Hurtubise.

Seventeen years of painting have awarded him, to-day, the precise vision of what he desires and the scale of his measure. At thirty-eight years of age, this taciturn man has a thinking hand, so true is it that painting begins where language ends, to say what the verb hardly portends.

Hurtubise heard the great voices of Pollock and De Kooning for a long time — and suffered the temptation of the strength of the gesture and orgiastic colour and, with an adolescent ardour, he sought to express his effervescent feeling in the face of life, sun, waves and forest. Then nature's dictionary fascinated him. He discovered structures, forms, laws; and the fine arts school, the teachers he had chosen, little by little directed his desires. Action painting and gestural painting helped him to find his own interior measure, the geometry of his space, while preserving harshness and sumptuous tones (acid pinks and electric greens), the spontaneous gush of colour.

The principal step in the disciplines imposed on his freedom is found at the moment when he decided to divide his pictures into a series of equal, interchangeable squares. In this way, he was able not only to assemble, juxtapose, remove the elements to arrive at the discovery of maximum intensity, but with perfect unity he introduced two essential values into his plastic development: a structured texture, a sort of mathematical quality that gives a meaning to his compositions and even to his inspiration, a genuine ossification, but at the same time he compelled himself to a profound play, a capacity of improvisation and of infinite combinations. He explained himself very plainly on this point. "I can change as many squares as I wish as I go along. If a part of a picture does not satisfy me, instead of destroying the picture I change only the elements with which I do not agree. I can thus experiment with collage, juxtapositions, assemblages, a very great number of concrete, sensitive and immediate possibilities. The work is the outcome of a permanent construction."

By instinct Hurtubise had discovered the fundamental law of great painting, the definition of a geometry bearing organic forms, born of the instinct to live. The blob, expression of impulse, of the poetic gift, of chance, of the ejaculation of the whole being, of the tension of the eye seizing reality, finds its true dynamics in a simple order that organizes it in a spiritual

space. And curiously, it was from Mondrian — thought of
again in order to better serve his personal gesture — that Hurtubise borrowed the great lesson of space without depth, the
contrast of colours, the cutting out of canvas. But he dared what
none of the disciples of the great Hollander of the school of
Paris had attempted: the real division of the canvas; and even
more, a monumental construction through the accumulation
of rhythmic effects. To-day his audacity allows him to project the
spontaneity of his arabesques and of his harshness of lines on
the largest possible space with an equilibrium of absolute purity.
His hazards have caught up with the necessity of the work. In
his compositions, a great balance, which I would call classic, fascinates the gaze. And even when he composes a canvas on
several axes, with a sure hand he finds the quality of an admirable occupation of space. Hurtubise is the creator of a geometry
in tension whose planes are charged with a violent energy that
sets off a poetic, mutable discharge. He introduces us into a
lucid irrationality and reveals to us a dimension of our modern
space that carries us beyond our usual perception.

    We often date the birth of modern art from the
Impressionists who cast out black from their palettes in order
to better record the vibrations of light on the landscapes they
wanted to apprehend in all the nuances of perception. In this
way they fixed the last moments of the ending rural world at the
same time as the first effects of this era of energy that char-
acterizes the twentieth century. An impressionist picture is a historical beacon from which one has the feeling of the passing of
history between yesterday and to-day. Until Fauvism, black had
disappeared like a symbol of mourning that one puts aside to
make way for life. But since that time it has not ceased to command attention. Cézanne, already, became angry at its disap-
pearance and his teaching was heard. All major painting, to find
its structure, assimilates the force of sensibility, fixes values,
demands the presence of black. The modern eye has banished
chiaroscuro and has re-established the power of black. On
my arrival in Montreal exactly one century after the last Impressionist exhibition, I found myself face to face in the street with
a poster that caught my eye, whose cadenced harshness proclaimed in black the power of a paraph. Street art, live, sure of its
conquests, signed Hurtubise.

    Laurent Lamy, who knows the painter well and
has seen him work a great deal, has recalled this adventure in
black in Hurtubise's painting: "On a background he then applies
as many as forty layers of shiny black, of an absolute unifor-
mity. A lesson in method, in meticulousness, that he gives himself. And, suddenly, after these hours of delicate polishing, in
a single, impetuous gesture he inscribes on these geometric fields
a sinuous white line. Brutally he symbolically destroys what
does not resemble him. With a ray of light he tears this black,
claws it, denies it." These signs are such as do not deceive.
They add themselves to so many indications on the value of a
development.

    His contained violence, his sensitive concentration,
the power of the antagonisms that he controls and with which
he plays, his brilliant gifts as a colourist and his strident or exquisite harmonies, the dissonant order that inspires him, all make
of Hurtubise one of the future greats of to-day's painting.

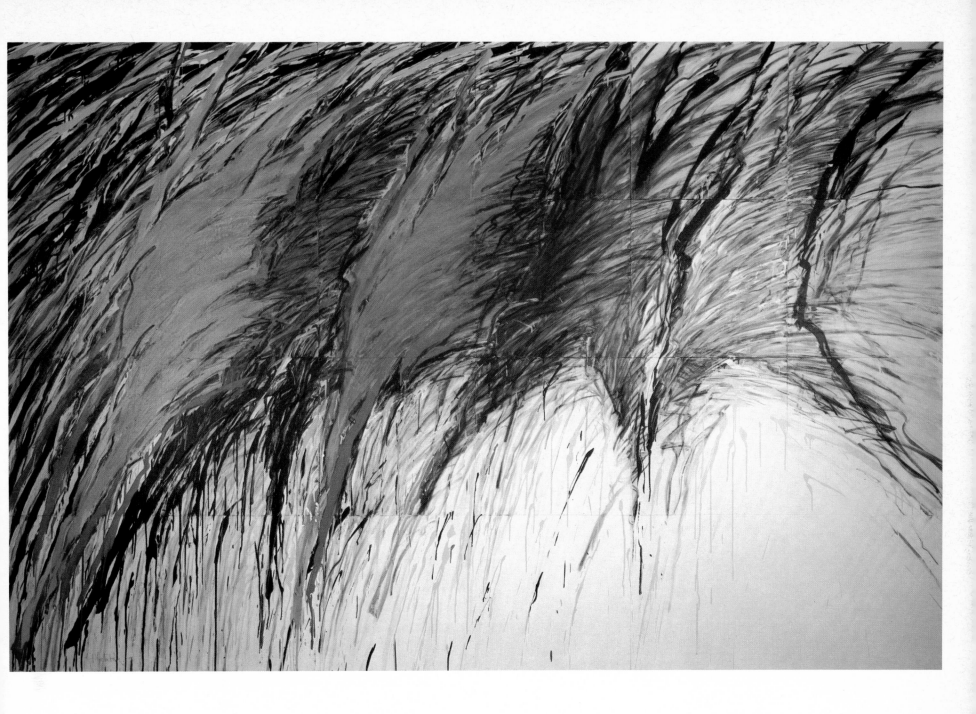

JACQUES HURTUBISE   BIOGRAPHICAL NOTES

Born in Montreal in 1939, Jacques Hurtubise studied at the Montreal Fine Arts School from 1956 to 1960 under Albert Dumouchel, Jacques de Tonnancour and Jean Simard. He was awarded a scholarship by the Max Beckmann Foundation and resided in New York from September 1960 to May 1961. He was a teacher of plastic arts under the Catholic School Commission of Montreal from 1961 to 1965. In 1965, he was chosen to represent Canada at the Eighth International Biennial at São Paulo, Brazil. He was invited to be artist in residence at Dartmouth College, New Hampshire, in 1967; he participated in the ninth and tenth São Paulo biennials in 1967 and 1968. In 1970, he received a grant from the Canada Arts Council. In 1971, he was named a member of the Royal Academy of Canada. In 1972 the Montreal Museum of Contemporary Art and the Quebec Museum organized a retrospective of his work. In 1975, he was selected to produce a serigraph for the Container Corporation of America at Chicago. Since 1976 he has been a professor at the University of Ottawa. His works are found in the important museums of Canada.

SELECTED BIBLIOGRAPHY

1961   Pierre Saucier, *Jeunes artistes au travail*, in *Vie des Arts*, Vol. V, No. 22, p. 43.

1965   Claude Jasmin, *Toccate et fugues de Molinari, Hurtubise et Tousignant sur des air connus*,
        in *La Presse*, Montreal, May 29.

1966   Fernande Saint-Martin, *Lettre de Montréal*, in *Art International*, February, pp. 47-48.

1970   Laurent Lamy, *Jacques Hurtubise*. Preface by Bernard Teyssèdre. Lidec, *Panorama* Collection.
        Montreal; *Hurtubise — Peintre de la clarté violente*, in *Vie des Arts*, Vol. XV, No. 59, p. 18-19.

1972   Catalogue of the *Hurtubise* Exhibition. Introduction by Laurent Lamy. Quebec Museum.

1973   *Jacques Hurtubise*. Éditions Yvan Boulerice, Montreal, 21 pages.
        Fernande Saint-Martin, *Hurtubise parle . . .*, in *Ateliers* (Montreal Museum of Contemporary Art),
        February 2.
        Françoise Arès, *L'Évolution d'Hurtubise, au Musée d'Art Contemporain*, in *Le Devoir*, Montreal,
        February 10, p. 20.
        Gilles Toupin, *Ces tableaux à noms de femmes*, in *La Presse*, February 10, p. D14.

1974   Gilles Toupin, *Hurtubise et les transes de l'Amérique*, in *La Presse*, October 26.

JAQUE

Monique BRUNET-WEINMANN

The painter questions. It is the poet who is in possession of the beginning of the answers. When the poet takes over from the painter he puts his symbolical world into words, and it is enough to listen to these words to find, better than in spoken ones, the Ariadne's thread of his interior labyrinth, the few first images which, developed, unfolded, enlarged, multiplied with all their variants, make up this ice palace that is the work, projection — reflections of the unique and universal being that founds it and that it founds. In 1976 Louis Jaque published *Dialogues parallèles*[1], roughed out some twenty years before, foreknowledge of a theme to which the pictorial work bears witness, just as one of the first drawings, *Vues de ma fenêtre* (1952), carries the germ of plastic evolution. These lines trace the self-portrait of a personal cosmography.

Soliterre. Solitary land at the heart of the galaxies, with years of dazzling light from nearby constellations; "solid" and "land" in rhyme[2] both in physics and in the zodiacal sign as obvious as a signal; brown ochre earths manipulated, kneaded with the sensual pleasure given by intimate contact with primordial material for future shaded colours on virgin canvas; earthy textures in which progressively the paint takes off for sidereal translucidities; solitude that comes to maturity apart from schools and theoretical discussions taken up again in chorus or distorted in weakened echoes. The impact of two words forges a new word, *soliterre,* that flashes with all the impressions left by the encounter with Louis Jaque and his work.

Seeing him come forward with the natural ease of one who is in his own home and daily environment, against the light, it seemed to me that Rodin's *Balzac* was slowly approaching: a massive figure, assurance reinforced by the pose of a certain proud indolence which, forgotten during the interview, allowed his face to show the real nobility of a direct look, astonishingly changing, expressive, mobile, betraying an ardour restrained through caution or modesty. Rarely can one see the mark of an astrological sign in the density of a personality. Balzac helped me in this evidence: Taurus. A gouache of 1961, *Tauromachie,* in which technical mastery is asserted — the dramatic lyricism of a red spatter on the earth tones and the deep black setting apart a small, clean square, the closed sign of a defence to be penetrated — and proves to be revealing: date of birth, the first of May.

At work, resemblance to a model for a statue is accentuated when the painter puts on a sort of aviator's jumpsuit dotted with multicoloured stains, just as significant as the monk's robe of the novelist; disguises do not mask, they reveal. With left hand on hip he carefully kneads the thick paint into a homogenous mixture: white, crimson, sanguine, lemon yellow, black, umber, to make a graduation of colours dominantly earthy. Oil, the solvent chosen because it dries slowly, brings it

about that his painting is first a tactile matter: he must create the desired consistency, malleable, supple, oily, corresponding to a certain brilliance and then rapidly with firm, precise gestures he must spread it in shaded, smooth layers on the support. Then the hand, which has laid hold, in the whole collection of carefully arranged and cleaned rollers, of the most appropriate to the stage in work (left hand still resting on hip), in an unflagging series of energetic back and forth movements, glues the material, improves the changing of values, modulates the interpenetration of the hues, iridescent grays and translucid blacks, creates for the eye all the radiances of surface, from blinding brilliance of intensity to velvety luminescence of shadows.

It remains to transform this light into space, to act so that the canvas, which already escapes flat bidimensionality through the play of directions founded on volumes and depth, digs for itself parallel planes, undulates, winds scrolls around a spiral, unrolls supple cones that open on the infinite void of interstellar space, a magnetic field animated by tensions and vibrating impulses.

It would be useless to bring this space back to the vast expanses of the plains, to the fields of snow or to the immensity of the sea, to memories experienced of limitless horizons: their sequence is actually not horizontal but vertical. The idea of landscape, even "abstract landscapism", according to an expression dear to Michel Ragon, would distort the poetic value and the spiritual implication of this work. Such an interpretation would lead to saying that man-centre-of-the-world is quite banished from it, that emotional warmth is cruelly lacking at the heart of this infinite, icy universe, open on despair. It would be unjust toward the man, for even if Louis Jaque, a solitary worker, holds himself apart from artistic groups, he lives surrounded, profoundly attached to the warm memory of the family milieu of his childhood and is essentially an optimist.

The aesthetic misinterpretation would be more serious. Indeed, the material that he exploited a great deal at his beginnings, the pictorial material from which, inevitably, he departs each time he undertakes a canvas, is no longer there when the picture emerges, except to give the illusion of its reverse, its opposite: weightlessness, antimatter, energy, in a word: light. Not in the restrained, still terrestrial sense of a luminous source providing lighting, this source being solar and the lighting being the full noon of the Impressionists: the pure light that Dante had so much trouble suggesting and shading for the ascension to the successive heavens of his Paradise, the light within oneself that interplanetary voyages will help us to imagine. This means that, for Louis Jaque, colours and forms are only the supports that allow attaining this supreme end by means of the lightening of values. This very subtle art excludes the imperfections that the charm of bright colour allows to pass and, sometimes, even integrates like so many happy accidents. It demands mastery, like the drawing in black and white, to which finally it is very close. We are fascinated by the noble harmony of certain canvases all in dark but not opaque tones, where the almost blacks and the opalescent grays transfigure the white, and bring to mind the famous paradox that the greatest colourists are those who paint in black and white. It is logical, also, that in spite of technical differences comparison with Seurat should have occurred and been maintained: light above all, the relief that makes volumes turn, the accuracy of shading that sets dimensions, space, retinal impression of vibrations and of maximum brilliance . . . A comparison justified by Louis Jacque, who admits having been captivated a few years ago in Paris by a Seurat drawing showing a back view silhouette in the misty light of the banks of the Seine. A confession of fraternity: "That is a drawing I would like to have made."

He substitutes "atmospheric perspective for linear perspective, slave of form, replaces geometric and divisible space by an opening on the boundless expanse that no longer allows itself to be enclosed or confined, but lures the eye into a dizziness. The world of the earth, which held complete sway, yields its rank to the sky (. . .) which becomes more and more the very milieu of painting"[3]. In short, I have the impression, after seeing him work, that Louis Jaque freshly assumes, for each new canvas in the creative practice, this important crossing from the classical to the baroque era such as René Huyghe defines it, a passing from a priority of form to that of light that effects a rectification of vision, substitutes vertically for horizontality, the cosmic void for earthly matter. Indisputably, he has remade it on his own account in the course of his personal development during a quarter of a century of painting. In a rapid glance, let us try to see how[4].

Until the turn of the sixties, Louis Jaque had almost exclusively used gouache, exploiting all its resources in texture to the maximum degree through crushing, teaseling, superimposition, spreading by roller, thanks to which he brings to perfec-

tion the originality of his present technique. He plays with the effects of material: harsh roughness of stone, granular fineness of sand, porosity, rock pitted by rust, ribs, woody veins, wood fibres, liquefaction of precious metals whose concentrated fusion resolves itself into light. By dint of manipulation, he succeeds in producing energizing waves, vibratory streaks, propulsion of fibres, to prove that finally the material blocks the surface. With *Radiances cosmiques No 1* (1964) he effects the synthesis and the liquidation of remotely figurative forms, scenic and horizontal, while, in the very centre of the picture, still closed and developing, the centrifugal verticalities of the shadings of tones command attention. Then the clean sweep, the blank page for appearances unsuspected outside of this arched *Radiance bleue,* the picture of interior liberation that tries to simplify "the man that was". A difficult simplification: tensions, conflicts, duality are translated into double forms that are separated or united, schisms or encounters, when the solar pendulum of *Signe de midi* (1966) strikes, to imbalance cleverly applied, almost vertical, exact and divided. It is necessary to go through rainbows which, to the abundance of their prismatic colours, add the complexity of the contradictions between their direction and that of the impulses that animate them, in order that finally white can definitely assert itself, a median luminescence that attracts in its centre, captivates and captures. Then it is that Louis Jaque attains what, until now, seems to me the best of his work, with the *Intradorsale* and *Noumènes spatiodynamiques* series (1970-1972).

Abstract painting par excellence, since it has the ambition of rendering the immaterial, the intangible, the idea of light, even when using blacks that are usually the symbol of heavy mass; it is also the opposite of conceptual art: like Leonardo's sfumato, the shadings of Louis Jaque's colours appeal to sensitivity, to dreaming rather than to thought, to the spiritual and not to the intelligence. But in his recent works, he escapes the baroque adherence of which one might be led to think by this partiality for light and the spirituality whose sign it traditionally is. By very structured diptychs and triptychs, which dictate to the eye a perpetual play of reflections and counterpoints, of "parallel dialogues" of lines, of continuity and breaks difficult to grasp, he restructures the expanse and emphasizes his vertical linear perspective: all these false parallels meet in infinity, in one point of flight projected into the cosmic dimension, the "metacentre", to go back to the lovely title of an older suite. This was the way the poets of the end of the Middle Ages imagined God, after the theologians, among whom was Nicolas de Cues, who had stated the famous definition: God is a sphere whose centre is everywhere, whose circumference is nowhere, a metacentre. The painter's trajectory proves to be transcendental, a spiritual asceticism propelling the *soliterre* into *L'Espoir galaxique.*

1. Album of seven poems and seven serigraphs. Montreal, Éditions Bourguignon.
2. Fourth Dialogue: . . . longing for you
   boreal chromatic gaze
   of your cycle of reflections
   nested in the ether
   infinitely more solid
   than an earthbound cathedral.
3. René Huyghe, *L'Art et l'âme.* Paris, Flammarion, 1960, p. 95.
4. A survey made possible by the exhibition at the Montreal Fine Arts Museum, from September 9 to October 9, 1977.

LOUIS JAQUE   BIOGRAPHICAL NOTES

The fifth of seven children, Louis Jaque was born in Montreal on the first of May, 1919. The family ambiance developed in him, naturally, as it were, a great interest in art: books on the history of art and on the aesthetics in the library at home were picture books and also the chief sources of his education, since he left school at the age of sixteen to enter the École du Meuble, which had just been opened. His teachers of drawing were Jean-Paul Lemieux, then Borduas, "who had not yet arrived". The history of art courses of Maurice Gagnon, who had just left the Sorbonne and the École du Louvre, gave him, as early as 1935-1938, a knowledge of contemporary European painting, and he went in this way from the plastic world of Ozias Leduc and Suzor-Coté to that of Mondrian.

During the war, Louis Jaque was an officer in an armoured division; so he crossed Canada from coast to coast from 1940 to 1945. Especially, for courses in camouflage, he had the opportunity to view the earth from above, deeply interested as he had been since childhood in flying and in the exploits of the first aviators: a determinative experience for his future direction. Demobilized, drawing forced itself upon him as an outlet to an engrossing work as designer, then gouache, from 1952. Louis Jaque was a professor first at the Institute of Applied Arts, then at the Old Montreal CEGEP.

SELECTED BIBLIOGRAPHY

1958 Paul Gladu, in *Le Petit Journal*, Montreal, November 2.
Rodolphe de Repentigny, in *La Presse*, Montreal, November 8.

1962 Guy Robert, *Louis Jaque, la magie de la gouache*, in *Vie des Arts*, Vol. VII, No. 28, pp. 28-33.

1963 Jacques Folch-Ribas, *Louis Jaque*, in *Vie des Arts*, Vol. VII, No. 30, p. 42.

1965 Laurent Lamy, in *Le Devoir*, Montreal, May 8.
Rea Montbizon, *The Cool and the Intimate*, in *The Montreal Gazette*, May 8.
Paul Gladu, *Louis Jaque, un peintre qui joue avec les soleils*, in *Le Petit Journal*, Montreal, May 16.

1966 Claude Jasmin, in *La Presse*, May 21.
Louis Jaque, Catalogue for the exhibition at the Museum of Contemporary Art, 4 pages.

1968 Rita Simon, *Louis Jaque*, in *Arts Magazine*, New York, June.

1969 *Art in New York*, in *Time Magazine* (American edition), October 31.

1970 Alain Hogue, *Le Beau par des effets magiques*, in *Le Soleil*, Quebec, March 14, p. 43.
Terry Kirkman, *Calm amidst the Turmoil*, in *The Montreal Star*, August 15, p. 8.
Irene Heywood, *Discovery . . . Canadian Style, Osaka. Quebec, Land of Opportunity* in
    Vie des Arts, Vol. XV, No. 59, pp. 54-57.

1971 Lorenza Trucchi, in *Momento-Sera*, Rome, March 13.
Henry Galy-Carles, in *Les Lettres françaises*, Paris, March 17.
Paul Dumas, *Le Peintre Louis Jaque à la Galerie de l'Apogée de Saint-Sauveur-des-Monts*, in
    L'Information médicale et paramédicale, October 19, p. 40.

1973 Massimo Javolella, *A propos d'une exposition de Louis Jaque à Milan*, in *Vie des Arts*, Vol. XVIII,
    No. 72, p. 75.

1975 Henry Galy-Carles, *Louis Jaque et l'univers cosmique*, in *Vie des Arts*, Vol. XX, No. 80, pp. 56-59.

1977 Yves Robillard, *La Santé avant tout*, in *Le Jour*, Montreal, September 16.
Jean-Claude Leblond, *Après 25 ans, une réflexion*, in *Le Devoir*, September 16.
René Viau, *Louis Jaque, un cheminement en perpétuel devenir*, in *La Presse*, September 17.

LEDUC

Jean-Pierre DUQUETTE

A large house of the last century, with red brick corners, a former presbytery adjoining a picturesque little church that hesitates between Romanesque and Gothic styles: it is here, at the entrance of a small town — almost a hamlet — that Fernand Leduc has been living for some years. From the autoroute leading to Chartres we see on the right the square, squat bell-tower that marks this point of the Beauce plain where the Leducs have elected to live. The church no longer has its own priest, but a time-switch faithfully sets off at noon and in the evening the angelus rung by the only bell with the tolling of another age. A local legend has it that a whole network of secret passages runs through the cellars toward the cathedral, a vestige of times troubled by religious wars and other revolutionary movements. Be this as it may, we can discern, from the windows of the attic transformed into a comfortable living room, the spires of Notre-Dame de Chartres that stand out on the horizon of wheat fields as in Charles Péguy's poem.

Two sides of the property incessantly remind us of the religious setting: a dividing wall that outlines the little cemetery on the south and a whole side of the church, of stones turned green by moss. Thérèse and Fernand Leduc have completely restored this property abandoned for decades. When they arrived here, the garden was like a virgin forest, invaded from all directions: the fruit trees back in the wild state, bushes growing out of control, the framework of a dilapidated bower quietly rusting away in the dampness of undergrowth. The house had a sad look from being so long uninhabited. A bonfire burned in the yard several weekends, fed by all kinds of trash, including old tires that gave off an enormous cloud of black, noisome smoke into the village sky. This near-ruin has become the ark of friendship. Behind the house, set slightly back, stands the studio, under a translucid glass roof from which falls a great even light, sometimes somewhat gray, sometimes somewhat golden, according to the condition of the sky and the time of the day. Cats walk about, doze, chase each other suddenly, chat with their mistress who adores them. It is here, in this rustic setting, away from the noise and the bustle of Paris, that the long, patient pictorial research begun in Montreal in the forties continues.

Claude Gauvreau, in an article in May 1950 on the occasion of a Leduc-Riopelle exhibition at the Galerie Creuze in Paris, no doubt drew the most accurate portrait of Leduc when he called the artist "this severe and slow seeker, so uncompromising, so meticulous, so pitiless toward himself"; he completed his sketch a few paragraphs later when he emphasized "the modesty and the almost legendary rectitude of this developing painter". There indeed is Leduc's profound personality, under the sign of absolute intellectual honesty. This is perhaps also what explains the fact that the evolution of his work knows no gaps, no sudden passing from one manner to another, but rather that it advances, as in an uninterrupted continuity, from the automatist accident of the beginnings to the secret, underlying construction of to-day's microchromies. Not that Fernand Leduc is an austere or rigid man. He experiences abrupt amazements, sudden enthusiasms and youthful bursts of laughter that sweep you along and raise you up; he also feels violent, uncontrollable indignation, against which it would be useless to protest. The *scrubbing* of Chartres' stained-glass windows, for instance, finds in him a fierce, obstinate opponent.

A walk along the fields where autumn ploughing has traced long, parallel furrows as far as the eye can see. The earth, turned over in thick, dark brown clumps, is hardened by December cold. Immense clouds move slowly in a slate-coloured sky. Pheasants fly off heavily along the thickets as you pass and make you start suddenly. What are we talking about? Everything, nothing; of a project of a monograph on the painter's work, which will finally be completed; of the winter, which seems well under way; of Borduas; of this Beauce plain, where "the deep swell and the ocean of wheat" have rustled in the east wind for centuries. Péguy sang about this Beauce earth beautifully: "Two thousand years of labour made this earth / A bottomless reservoir for new ages". A landscape at one time attractive, fascinating and implacable in its uninterrupted flatness. "The country is flatter than the flattest table. Hardly a hollow in the earth, hardly a little fold/. It is the judge's table and the accomplished fact, / And the stop without appeal and the inevitable order." Is this truly chance? Is it a conjuncture of the stars that led Thérèse and Fernand Leduc here, to the heart of this plain, into this big house where life flows evenly at the will of the seasons, in this age-old light? This house where all year long friends flock, French as many as Quebecer, for a weekend or a week, certain that affection, endless discussions, dishes cooked in a flash, as if by magic, and the local wine will not be wanting.

Back from the walk. Apple tree logs flame in the fireplace; it is time for hot toddy or whiskey.

But after all, why France? this *exile* that some in Quebec still feel is an anomaly, indeed an insult. That is a question which, for so many years that it has been asked them, finally, and with some reason, exasperates the Leducs. In February 1947,

Fernand joined Thérèse, who had preceded him to Paris; he also met Riopelle there and organized the first exhibition of Montreal automatists at the Galerie du Luxembourg, in June-July. This first stay in France would last until spring 1953. For a young painter, to-day as formerly, it is only normal to go and work and live abroad, in great centres such as Paris or New York, where all aesthetic experiments converge, crucibles where the artist finds himself located at the junction of the principal trends and the newest movements of an era. And we must not forget that, since the appearance of *Refus global* at the end of summer 1948 Fernand Leduc had, himself, gone beyond the automatist experiment and was penetrating further into his research, at a time when accident and the spontaneous gesture in part from Surrealism were to give place little by little to a more thoughtful structuralization and to a more and more constructed arrangement of pictorial matter.

The Leducs returned to Montreal in 1953. On several occasions, Leduc returned to the teaching that he had practised before his departure. In 1959, he went again to France, where he has since been living, with regular trips back to Quebec. All in all, he has therefore chosen to live in France, but he is no less a Quebecer, as is his wife. This a personal choice, a decision which deeply concerns only the interested persons themselves. This absence, in which some would like to see a sort of betrayal, boils down to physical distance, purely and simply. And, in any case, the Leducs are not the only artists or writers from here who usually live abroad. In April 1970 Leduc told Guy Viau: "In France I feel at home. This allusive way of thinking, all in nuances. There is in me something very deep in that sense, following the dialogue at the interior. And yet my associations of colours are imported, are of my country, but transposed. Here, people are sometimes astonished that it was done in France. In Canada, they find it is French. . . ."

It was in France that Fernand Leduc would know one of the most profound — and rare — influences in the evolution of his aesthetic ideas, after the disappointing meeting with André Breton. In *Interview transatlantique,* the article mentioned above which appeared in *Le Haut Parleur* of Montreal in May 1950, Claude Gauvreau reproduces the following passage from a letter that Leduc wrote to him: "The acquaintance with Raymond Abellio was and remains for me the most enriching contact of my stay in France. I am still on the threshold of a spiritual adventure that seems to me of an inexhaustible breadth." At the end of 1948 already, in a letter in which he commented on the manifesto that had appeared the previous summer — signed by Leduc "in the freedom and security of Paris", as Gauvreau would write later (we must come back to this one day soon) — Leduc said to Borduas: "And so, in opposition to the crushing moralizing atmosphere, we believed we had to rely on *desire* and *passion* while giving these terms a wider and wider meaning without realizing that it involved, rather than desire and passion, a superior aspiration (an appeal to the mind) of our soul toward unity. . . . Likewise anarchy and revolution; it is rather a matter of hierarchy and evolution (in harmony)." And Leduc would speak in subsequent letters of his discovery of Abellio's thought, to which Borduas replied on January 6, 1949: "Spirituality? This word worries me: the old habit of coming out from man's nature to meet God, the angels and all past torments. This word is bursting with millenial dreams. I am lacking mystery-

objectives. To that word I prefer this one, which has its beginning and its end in man, the little brother of everything that may be; a word full of substance and action. You will be startled: Automatism." A few weeks later, in another letter, Borduas came back to this, explaining that he could not hold to a "spiritual universe", "an exacting and noble" road, on account of his "passion" and his (historic) "reason". Nonetheless, on March 22, 1949 he told Leduc, who had sent him *Vers un nouveau prophétisme:* "I understand and share your admiration, dear Fernand."

It still remains to define precisely all the elements of Leduc's discovery as well as Borduas' final reaction a few months later: "No, definitely, it's no good any longer, Mr. Abellio!" Not that this letter marks a breach between them: it is addressed to (His) "dear Fernand", and Borduas in ending it sends him his "Fraternal greetings". All this suggests to what point Abellio's thoughts marked the evolution of Fernand Leduc, who had finally broken with the Surrealists in June 1947 with a letter in fairly heretical terms for any strictly observant Surrealist: "I understand Surrealism as well with, without or even against Breton, but one must in any case formulate one's unceasing renewal, without which the ambiguous cannot be cleared up."

For anyone who knows Leduc, ideas of balance and harmony are not surprising. His very character would already reveal this to us, as we have seen: between extreme reactions and contradictions he appears constantly in search of an order, an ideal of measure that would reconcile the opposite tendencies profoundly ingrained in him. In his penetrating article of *La Barre du jour* on the automatists, Bernard Teyssèdre has expressed this in one sentence: "shielded between badly differentiated tendencies, Leduc is able with the same impulse to celebrate the unconscious and the conscious, the spontaneous and the considered, the lawless and the ordered, the excessive and the lightly suggested." And speaking of his work in 1944-1945, he wonders to what point this position, not of *exact centre* but of *balance through compensated excesses* could be maintained. The result of Leduc's work is the most enlightening answer that can be made to this question. In fact, we shall see in it a clearer and clearer organization of form, an abstraction more and more constructed in geometrical planes, in a simplification and a more marked economy of means, going so far as the extreme stripping down of *composition, passage* and *erosion* of the sixties. At present, form itself is eliminated from the surface of the microchromies, to produce a single restoration of light. And, at the same time, colour has become reduced to binary chromatics, to the appearance of monochromatics in the last pictures. Research for harmony which flows into extreme purification, on a simplification that borders on vertigo.

About two years ago, Fernand Leduc told me in an interview: "I dream now of capturing the special qualities of the gray light of this region, the fogs of Champseru and the Beauce plain." In the catalogue of a recent exhibition at the Canadian Cultural Centre in Paris (April-June 1977) René Le Bihan very precisely defines this step which tends to "erase the constructed picture" and that, by so doing, Leduc "meets radical preoccupations of current painting that aspires to nothing less than raising its means and restoring its domain". Exigence and patience in thought are not qualities lacking in Fernand Leduc. Somewhere near Chartres he pursues with enthusiasm the stubborn quest begun twenty years ago.

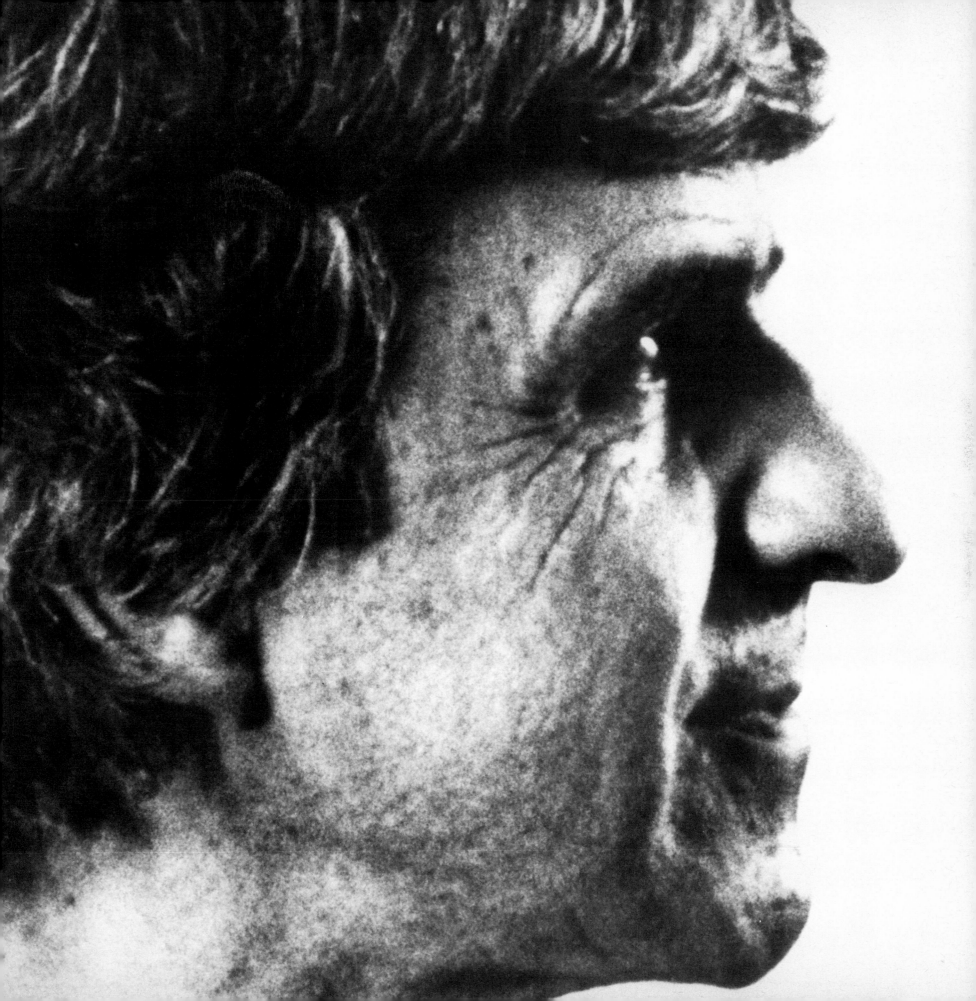

FERNAND LEDUC   BIOGRAPHICAL NOTES

Fernand Leduc was born in Montreal on July 4, 1916. In 1939 he enrolled in the Montreal School of Fine Arts and in 1943 received his teaching certificate in drawing. From 1942 to 1953 he taught this subject in the Montreal Catholic School Commission, at Notre Dame College and at Saint-Denis College in Montreal. He took part in the founding and the exhibitions of the Group of Automatists from 1942 to 1950. From 1947 to 1953 he resided for the first time in France and participated in several exhibitions, among which was *Automatisme* at the Luxembourg Gallery. Upon his return to Montreal, with Molinari, Tousignant, Juneau and Toupin, he joined the Plasticians' movement. In 1956 he founded the Montreal Association of Non-Figurative Artists. He again lived in France from 1959 to 1970 and became a member of the Salon des Réalités Nouvelles in Paris (1965-1970), as well as of the Salon Comparaisons (1969-1970). In 1969 he received honourable mention at the International Festival of Painting at Cagnes-sur-Mer (France). From 1970 to 1972, he taught at the Arts Department of the University of Quebec at Montreal, then at the Quebec Fine Arts School and, finally, at the Visual Arts School of Laval University. Fernand Leduc usually lives in France.

SELECTED BIBLIOGRAPHY

1962   Catalogue of the *Grands formats* Exhibition. Presented by Pierre Descargues, Galerie Hautefeuille, Paris.

1966   Catalogue of the *Fernand Leduc* Exhibition at the Quebec Museum. Preface by Guy Viau.

1969   Bernard Teyssèdre, *Fernand Leduc, peintre et théoricien du surréalisme à Montréal (1941-1947)*, *La Barre du Jour*, Montreal, Nos. 17-20.

1970   Catalogue of *Introduction: Fernand Leduc*. Presented by Guy Viau. Travelling exhibition (1970-1971) organized by the National Gallery of Canada and the Canadian Cultural Centre, Paris.
       Noël Lajoie, *Fernand Leduc*, in *La Revue des Deux-Mondes*, No. 19.
       Bernard Teyssèdre, *Métamorphose en continuité de Fernand Leduc* in the catalogue of the Retrospective at the Museum of Contemporary Art, Montreal.
       Irene Heywood, *Ideas and Ideals from 20 Years Ago to To-day*, in *The Montreal Star*, December 26, p. 47.

1971   Laurent Lamy, *L'Itinéraire personnel de Fernand Leduc*, in *Vie des Arts*, Vol. XV, No. 62, pp. 30-35.
       Michel Ragon, *L'Automatisme québécois et les origines historiques de l'abstraction lyrique*, in *L'Art Vivant*, No. 24.

1973   Fernand Leduc, Éditions Yvan Boulerice, Montreal, 26 pages.

1974   Normand Biron, *Les 7 jours, Fernand Leduc*, in *Vie des Arts*, Vol. XVIII, No. 74, pp. 22-23.

1975   Michael Greenwood, *The Canadian Canvas*, in *Artscanada*, Nos. 196-197.

1976   Jean-Pierre Duquette, *De l'automatisme aux microchromies*, in *Voix et Images*. Vol. 2, No. 1.

1977   Catalogue of the *Microchomie, Gris puissance 6* Exhibition at the Canadian Cultural Centre, Paris. Interview with Fernand Leduc by Jean-Pierre Duquette; essay by René Le Bihan, curator of the Brest Museum.

LEMIEUX

Jean-Loup BOURGET

It is a paradox that in order to follow the St. Lawrence to its historic source, you must come down the river. Since it was discovered from the east, from the sea, you start at the end of the route traced by Jacques Cartier and Samuel de Champlain. In a manner of speaking, you also go from the 20th century (Montreal) to the 19th (Quebec) and even to the 18th century (the Isle-aux-Coudres). It is a journey made by Jean-Paul Lemieux himself. Having resided for a long time in Montreal, he withdrew to Quebec and for the past twenty or twenty-five years, he spends the greater part of the year, from April to November, on the island. A return to source, and an inner exile as well, going back to the essential task of painting and escaping from the social demands made on a famous artist who is a friend of all who matter in Quebec and the rest of Canada.

Lemieux is in a curious position, inasmuch as he has often been compared to, and even assimilated with, the expressionists, whilst being the least *expressive* of painters. His works have a controlled, reserved quality, a sensibility so acute that it distrusts itself and curls up like a snail recoiling before an obstacle. One of his favourite painters, it is true, is the Norwegian Munch, but Jean-Paul Lemieux' cry is, as it were, suffocated within, in spite of such explicit titles as *Le Chemin qui mène nulle part* or *Le Visiteur du soir* (both of 1956); there is even *L'Angoisse* (1967). Like the Fleming Ensor, Lemieux may be defined as an exile of the interior.

Munch, Ensor, Lemieux: these are men of the North, of a particular countryside, of a particular civilization. The distinction must be made between the setting of Quebec and that of the Ile-aux-Coudres, although they are united by the river, or rather, by the inner salt water sea of the St. Lawrence. First the city of Quebec itself, an admirable hybrid, an inspired union of site and architecture, of Anglo-Saxon and Gallic atmospheres (their common feature lies in their evocation of the Celtic fringe, in their homes, grey as in Scotland or Brittany, or vividly painted as in Ireland — well-rendered in *La Nuit à Québec-Ouest* (1964). It is a baroque-neo-classical blend (the Cathedral steeped in the gold of its piety and swarming with nuns), a garrison with a haughty citadel, a dwelling for middle-class families. It is a town that is home-loving and thus secret, and a tourist-attraction, hence open. Its plethora of hotels and restaurants conjures up Belgium, either directly, or indirectly, by way of Jean Ray's *Aventures de Harry Dickson,* stories frequently set in the English provinces. Quebec rococo, studded with church-towers, bell-turrets, lanterns and lantern-cages, Antwerp or Bratislava, is featured in *Église du Vieux Québec* (1955).

Going farther down the river, the houses are few and far between and a mixed landscape combines mountainous and aquatic features. The Laurentians slope towards the barren shore, the farmhouses have shingles (from Quebec on, the shop-windows are full of "Irish" and "Scottish" woollens . . .), worms for fishing are on sale everywhere. The silvery steeples glint in the sun, being both decorative and functional. They are protected against rust and the intemperate climate and serve as sign-posts for miles around, taut as bows against the sky. This is a country of marshy inlets, reminiscent — on a gigantic North American scale — of that other Celtic fringe, Cornwall, and the old church of St. Just in Roseland, for example, with its abrupt descent to the creek across which a majestic heron stalked. Some time ago, Jean-Paul Lemieux journeyed to London and South-West England, to Bath and to Stonehenge which dwarfs the rock-alignments at Carnac.

Lemieux explained to me that when he came to the island more than twenty years ago, he was plunged literally into the 17th century. There was the accent to start with; there were neither motor vehicle nor electricity. As Valéry remarked, islands are by nature the guardians of traditions. To-day, a semi-spontaneous, semi-touristic craftmanship flourishes; silhouettes of Jacques Cartier, the work of a local naive sculptor rise before us. There is a polychrome version in the Lemieux garden where a copse of russet hues is embraced by the fall. An owl stands on the terrace, itself a little citadel, like a fairy-tale commander, dominating the island shore and the river, opposite Gabrielle Roy's village. Lemieux has illustrated *La petite poule d'eau* (1971), and she has written a remarkable article about Lemieux[1]. A rust-covered cannon, salvaged from the sea, points up-river. Lemieux tells me with a smile that, according to Laurier, the last cannon-ball in defence of the British Empire was to be shot by a French-Canadian. Just now, on the well-tarred road, we passed a cart drawn by a miniature horse. To-day, however, the island is a precarious refuge. It is subject to peaceful invasions by the coming and going of the ferry which has replaced the former lighters (the Ile-aux-Coudres made its cinematic début at the same time as the Quebec cinema itself, fifteen years ago now, with Pierre Perrault's splendid documentaries: *Pour la suite du monde, Le règne du jour, Les Voitures d'eau, Un pays sans bon sens*).

Marcel Proust (a reference which I think Lemieux would approve of, given such titles as *1910 Remembered,* 1960, *Charlottetown Revisited,* 1964, *Été 1914,* 1965; *Dans le temps,* 1967) made the distinction in the word *place* names between the name and the place. Half-seriously, Lemieux deplores Jacques Cartier's lack of imagination; on landing here four and a half centuries ago, he saw a few hazel-nut trees and baptized the island "the Isle of the Hazelnut Trees". On the other hand, Champlain was the magician who gave names like "The Isle of the Geese", "The Isle of the Cranes" ... The wild geese, explains Lemieux, fly right over the roof of his house. I remember the day in London when, drawn by a strange cry, I rushed to the window: it was a flight of wild geese.

The interior of the house, which bears the mark of Madeleine Lemieux' taste for fine objects and jewels, has the slightly rugged gentleness of a familiar texture, of a tweed garment or of old wood, long and lovingly caressed. Pine furniture, so-called Portneuf pottery (which, as Madeleine Lemieux tells me, in fact comes from Scotland) with its vivid pink, mauve and carmine hues. A steeple cock, statues of the Virgin, crucifixes including one with raised arms which seems Jansenist, angels in adoration, some gilded, some plain. The absence of works by the painter is striking. Both inside and out, traditions are proclaimed, a rootedness in the little homeland — except for the numerous signs of the 20th century — central heating, the telephone, the New Yorker open on a low table. In all this, one is reminded of one of Lemieux's mentors — the Gauguin of the Yellow Christ.

Upstairs, there is a bedroom and the painter's studio. A huge canvas covers almost the entire wall. It is an official portrait of an important person, which will be unveiled soon. Aside from this major, twilight work, a few small paintings are modestly, even carelessly, turned against the wall. Landscape sketches with the Nordic character which Lemieux himself has so well defined "I use not colour, but shade".

In the living-room, however, there is a 1944 study for Fête-Dieu à Québec which sheds considerable light on Jean-Paul Lemieux and on his Quebec environment. Here again is the city of convents and church steeples, of lanes and alleyways, of sloping streets and stairways, an entire people, who for want of native emblems (before the fleur-de-lys flag was adopted by Duplessis) had recourse to symbols from elsewhere, without heed for contradictions. The French tricolour, symbol of a Revolution which shook the social and religious order, and the Pope's yellow and white colours: a dual fidelity, analogous perhaps to Lemieux' interpretation of the pontifical Zouaves shown in the painting. Whereas the latter defended the Pope in 1860, with Lamoricière, Quebec also welcomed those of her sons who had fought on the other side with Garibaldi. This contradictory procession, at once Catholic and Jacobin, this teeming life, the little figures in their festive and familiar setting cannot fail to evoke Ensor and his Christ's Entry into Brussels. And beyond that of course, one may go back as far as Brueghel.

To resume — inadequately but inevitably — Lemieux' expressionism, such as it is, and according to the degree of its interiorisation, relates less to the Scandinavian (Munch) or German (Nolde) brand, than to the surrealistic Belgian type, not only to Delvaux, whom Lemieux openly appreciates, but above all, to Degouve de Nuncques, with his seemingly blind architectural constructions in the undergrowth. One example of Degouve de Nuncques or Atkinson Grimshaw kinship might be found in the Anglican Cathedral of Quebec, whose tower, a replica of that of St. Martin in the Fields in London, is washed by moonlight between skeletal branches. Or again: Khnopff.

From a literary standpoint, Quebec's Bruges-la-Morte atmosphere may be noted, admirably treated by Lemieux in his Hommage à Nelligan (1971), reminding one of the portrait of Rodenbach by Lévy-Dhurmer. And also a painter beloved of Proust, Le Sidaner, an Impressionist of twilight, of mystery and of muted disquiet. Lovers of literary anecdotes might be interested in the following story. On leaving a party, Lemieux and another guest accidentally swap coats. The latter notices that he is wearing Lemieux' overcoat when he finds in the pocket Henry James' Portrait of a Lady.

Who was the fool that said "small countries, small minds"? The small countries are exemplary, because as in microcosms, one sees everything close up, enlarged, more clearly. This is true of Quebec, from which one painter chose flight, the gamble of the open, international market (Jean-Paul Riopelle), and another, the retreat into himself — Jean-Paul Lemieux. Nevertheless, like Flaubert, he has a royal chamber — the walls notwithstanding — which has not been destroyed, an imaginary museum, where Piero della Francesca and Edward Hopper, Monsu Desiderio and Nicolas de Staël are to be found, side by side.

In his life, Lemieux follows the seasons; he mischievously asks a politician who wants his portrait painted: "Do you want a summer-portrait? a winter one? spring or autumn? Winter? Very well. What do you wear in winter? Hatless? Really? Bareheaded, then. And your coat? A simple herring-bone tweed. All right, then, herring-bone, but a herring-bone is so tricky to paint ...

1. In Vie des Arts, Vol. VII, No. 29, pp. 38-43.

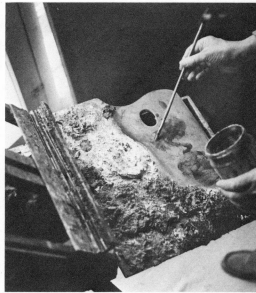

JEAN-PAUL LEMIEUX   BIOGRAPHICAL NOTES

Born at Quebec on November 8, 1904, Jean-Paul Lemieux enrolled in the Montreal School of Fine Arts in 1926. But soon he had to interrupt his studies to spend a year in Europe. Having graduated from the Montreal School of Fine Arts in 1934, he was named assistant professor at the same school, and then in 1935 became professor of drawing and painting at the École du Meuble before returning to Quebec in 1937 to teach at the School of Fine Arts, where he would be titular head of the course in painting until 1965. A grant from the Canada Arts Council in 1954 permitted him to return to Europe. Since 1965 he has lived in retirement, either at his house at Sillery or at the one at Ile-aux-Coudres, where he devotes himself exclusively to his activities in painting.

The artistic career of this painter has been the object of many marks of honour: in 1967 he received the medal of the Canada Arts Council and was named Companion of the Order of Canada. In 1970 he was awarded two doctorates honoris causa, one by Laval University (Quebec) and the other by Bishop University (Lennoxville). In 1971 he received the Philippe-Hébert Prize awarded by the Saint-Jean-Baptiste Society and in 1974 the Molson prize (Canada Arts Council). His works are to be found in the most important Canadian collections.

SELECTED BIBLIOGRAPHY

1938 Gérard Morisset, *En visitant l'exposition de M. et Mme Jean-Paul Lemieux*, in *Le Soleil*, Quebec, November 14.

1953 Gilles Corbeil, *Jean-Paul Lemieux, peintre intimiste*, in *Arts et Pensée*, Montreal, November.

1956 Claude Picher, *La Côte d'Azur*, in *Vie des Arts*, Vol. I, No. 2, pp. 24-25.
R.B., *Exposition de Jean-Paul Lemieux à l'Atelier*, in *L'Événement-Journal*, Quebec, March 2.

1957 Claire-P. Gagnon, *Le Peintre Jean-Paul Lemieux*, in *La Patrie*, Montreal, April 7.

1959 Rodolphe de Repentigny, *L'Art expressif et ambigu de Lemieux*, in *La Presse*, Montreal, March 19.

1962 Gabrielle Roy, *Les Terres Nouvelles de Jean-Paul Lemieux*, in *Vie des Arts*, Vol. VII, No. 29, pp. 38-43.

1963 Jacques Folch-Ribas, *Jean-Paul Lemieux et le trouble de la majesté*, in *Liberté*, Montreal, March.
Dorothy Pfeiffer, *Jean-Paul Lemieux*, in *The Montreal Gazette*, April 6.

1964 Gaston L'Heureux, *Jean-Paul Lemieux . . .*, in *Le Soleil*, November 28.

1967 Jean-Paul Lemieux, *Montreal Museum of Fine Arts*, 80 pages.
Yves Robillard, *Un homme devant le mouvement des choses*, in *La Presse*, September 16, p. 42.
Robert Ayre, *All the Lonely People*, in *The Montreal Star*, September 23.
Claude Daigneault, *Lemieux au Musée du Québec*, in *Le Soleil*, October 21.
Jean Royer, *Jean-Paul Lemieux au cœur du temps*, in *L'Action*, Quebec, October 21.
Kay Kritzwiser, *Touching Simplicity dominates Lemieux's Show*, in *The Toronto Globe and Mail*, December 9.

1968 Guy Robert, *Jean-Paul Lemieux, ou la poétique de la souvenance*, Éditions Garneau, Quebec, 140 pages.

1969 Marthe Morisset-Blackburn, *Jean-Paul Lemieux, peintre du temps muet*, in *Europe*, Paris, February.

1974 *Jean-Paul Lemieux*, Quebec, Ministry of Cultural Affairs, 79 pages.
Robert Lévesque, *Jean-Paul Lemieux et sa vision du pays*, in *Québec-Presse*, Montreal, June 23.
Raymond Vézina, *Le Cycle de la vie humaine*, in *Vie des Arts*, Vol. XIX, No. 77, pp. 20-25.

1975 Robert Marteau, *De l'immobilité vivante de Lemieux*, in *Le Jour*, Montreal, February 1.
Guy Robert, *Lemieux*. Les Éditions Internationales Alain Stanké, Montreal, 303 pages.

LETENDRE

Micheline MOISAN

"The works of an artist are influenced by his or her environment," said Rita Letendre recently in Toronto while taking us on a tour of the house where she and her husband, Kosso Eloul, have lived since 1974. Indeed, they have created for themselves an ideal space in which to work and live.

The house dates back to the second quarter of the nineteenth century, when the area south of Cabbage Town was developed. Rita delights in the fact that her home once belonged to the Parlows, a family of musicians. She and Kosso have succeeded in renovating the house while maintaining its original character. They endeavoured to unify the space and light; walls and the stairway have been knocked down, and a suspended staircase has been constructed. The woodwork and some brick walls have been stripped.

On the main floor, the kitchen and dining-room merge with a lovely conservatory also used as a breakfast nook and lounge. Plants and flowers abound but orchids, Rita's passion, predominate. The conservatory opens onto the courtyard-garden where, with the help of a student, Rita has constructed a small cement pond edged with flat stones. With her strong feeling for life, she has placed in it Japanese fish, a high papyrus plant and a tiny artificial waterfall. At the end of the courtyard stands a coach-house recently converted into a studio with a mezzanine. Rita transformed her former studio on the second floor of the main house into an office and drawing studio. She says that she found it impossible to draw in a room pervaded by sprayed acrylic.

This pleasant, comfortable and varied environment is vital to Rita's moral and physical well-being. She feels that "to be a good artist, it is necessary to be as complete a person as possible». For Rita, this comprehensiveness must take place in a single location. She devotes very much time to artistic creation but, during the day, she takes breaks to cook, do woodwork, look after the house, plants, fish and animals — Yaffa, the Doberman and Koshka, the Persian cat. She does everything with simplicity, effortlessness and joyful serenity.

Numerous works of art greatly contribute to the ambiance of the Sherbourne Street house. For this reason, Rita and Kosso refuse to part with some of them, particularly their own. Almost all by Rita's hand, the paintings present a survey, as it were, of the evolution of her style. It is a remarkably interesting development. The oldest works date from 1952, two years after Rita, who was then a student at the School of Fine Arts, experienced what she terms a "love at first sight" for works in the "scandalous" *Rebelles* exhibition which included paintings by Borduas. A few months later, Rita was to embark on the path of abstract art. The 1952 paintings are made up of little dabs of colour applied with the knife and, occasionally, with the brush. They relate to Automatism, although they are perhaps less dependent on spontaneity.

Three years later, she participated in the *Espace 55* exhibition held at the Montreal Museum of Fine Arts. In her paintings, while retaining their all-over quality, the pastel-coloured dabs have become larger and geometrically shaped. This change probably was influenced by Mondrian. In 1957, a further transformation is noticeable, as the now-smaller dabs waver and the all-over scheme is replaced by an emphasis on the centre of the composition.

Rita reverted to a certain spontaneity in 1958. The large, thick dabs applied all over the canvas and linked by the trails of the knife evoke Borduas, who was in Paris at the time, but had had an exhibition that May at the Galerie Agnès Lefort in Montreal.

It is especially from 1959 that Rita asserted her strong artistic personality. With smaller, thick and rather regular dabs of paint, she created highly structured paintings. The colours are few: black, which has the greatest importance, an unusual green, yellow, white and, sometimes, a dab of red as in *Chrysalide* (1959), a fine example in the collection of the Montreal Museum of Fine Arts. The tension created by the shapes and the expressive strength of the compositions link Rita to the Abstract Expressionist trend.

In the years 1963-64, a certain simplification appears: the coloured forms are less numerous and larger, and the paint is applied somewhat less heavily. However, the sense of conflict is still very strong. For instance, in Écho (1964, the artist's collection), a bright blue form is inserted in the black plane and struggles with it while, below, three earth-hued shapes enclose a yellow one endowed with a circular movement which resists the compression. In some paintings, one colour only — orange or red — struggles against the black. This production is intensely dramatic and one is not surprised to hear Rita say that it took place in an emotionally "tormented" time.

A period of residence in California in 1965 was to have a great influence on Rita's style. She and Kosso had been invited to participate in an international symposium at Long Beach College. Rita's contribution was Sunforce, a large mural on an outside wall above a busy campus passageway. The nature of the work — vast and far from the spectator — called for a simplified and monumental style. The technique was an innovation: epoxy, and Rita had to apply it with the long-forgotten brush. The composition is quite successful and recalls in a modified manner a couple of 1963 paintings in which a shape hurtling through space hits another shape, causing it to become fragmented by the impact. The 1963 hurtling form evokes in fact lightning and prefigures even more closely the present theme of the beam.

Another factor affecting Rita's style was the artist's initiation into the technique of printmaking, which subsequently took on much importance in her oeuvre. During the ten months the couple spent in Los Angeles, Rita, striving for a clarity of style, did not paint and worked only on silk-screen printing.

A profound change can be noted in the new acrylic paintings exhibited at the Galerie Agnès Lefort in the autumn of 1966. The large black and white canvases with their monumental, flattened shapes, are particularly noteworthy. The most characteristic theme is that of a polygonal form, a point of which is directed or poised on a secondary form, barely modifying it. This obviously refers to Sunforce, but without the impact and resulting fragmentation. We must, at this point, mention the possibility that the evolution of Rita's style may also be due to the influence of Kosso's sculpture, with its geometric and compact forms.

Two years later, the polygonal, active form has been transformed into an elongated triangle or dart, black and very precisely defined. Converging rays in light colours positioned alongside the black dart lend dynamism and luminous vibrations to the compositions. The placement of the beams may vary from horizontal to vertical to diagonal. It may also be doubled up. Occasionally, a slight divergence in the rays contributes a certain tension to the composition.

From that time, the beam became Rita's own theme, her personal mode of expression which she was to explore in a remarkable manner to this day. She endeavoured to intensify the dynamism and luminosity of her compositions. The black lines that she traced between the coloured darts reinforced the optical effects. Until 1970, she sometimes added metallic powders or ground mother of pearl to the acrylic, lending to works such as Lodestar (1970, Art Bank, Canada Council) an extraordinary opalescence. The colours became brighter and, in 1971, she began to replace the black demarcation lines with coloured ones, in-creasing their number to obtain a more shimmering effect. A few months later, for the same reason, she ceased to size her canvases. She experimented with the spray-gun and started using it instead of the brush to apply the colour between the peripheral rays. This change was gradual, almost imperceptible. "I like to make my way slowly," she says.

Toward 1974, the beam, particularly the black ray, became slimmer, while the hazy bands took on a greater importance. They deepened the space and generated subtler pulsations. More recently, they have taken on incandescent hues, as seen in the splendid Koshak (1976, The Montreal Museum of Fine Arts). Here the artist creates an interesting contrast between the fulgurating hard edge element and the atmospheric wide purple and red bands. With the duality, harmony is achieved.

In the house on Sherbourne Street, it is possible to study Rita's silk-screen prints in relation to her paintings. She has used the technique constantly since California. She claims that it has as much importance as her painting and enables her to express her creativity more completely. She adds that she is fascinated with the "marvelous transparencies", as well as with the technical difficulties of the medium.

Rita's environment is also her neighbourhood where she likes to stroll with Yaffa and chat with the shopkeepers, especially her orchid dealer. She is fond of walking and driving around the city, which she appreciates for its green spaces, its low pollution rate and its brick buildings, old and new. She and her husband first came to Toronto in 1968, after Kosso received a commission for a sculpture. They were so pleased with their stay that they returned often and finally settled there.

There is a particularly good reason for Rita to feel at home in the Queen City, since it has been enhanced by her art. She had, as we recall, proven herself as a muralist at Long Beach College in 1965. Consequently, it is not surprising to find her Sunrise of 1971 shining on the upper part of a lateral wall of Neill-Wycik College. Since 1972, Urtu has ornamented the side wall of an old house on Davenport Street. In addition, Rita's murals adorn the entrance halls of some apartment complexes. In 1976, the Royal Bank of Canada commissioned Irowakan for the plaza of its main office. Monumental wall painting is a technique to which Rita's style is very well attuned, with its strength, its sense of structure and its dynamism. It is exceptionally relevant in the contemporary urban environment.

The crowning touch of Letendre's urban contribution is Joy, the huge tempered glass ceiling vaulting the new Glencairn subway station. Executed in vivid colours, it is 180 feet long by 21 feet wide.

Rita Letendre, child of wanderers (she is descended from the Abenaki and Mohawk tribes), considers her environment with satisfaction and reflects, "I am fortunate". But we know very well that her "fortune" was forged, created by herself, as with all the rest.

113

RITA LETENDRE   **BIOGRAPHICAL NOTES**

Born in Drummondville in 1928, Rita Letendre studied at the Montreal School of Fine Arts. She took part in several demonstrations of the automatist group during the fifties. In 1962 she received a travelling grant from the Canada Arts Council and sojourned in France, Italy, Spain and Israel. From 1965 to 1970 she settled in Los Angeles, took courses in engraving and produced a mural for the California State College at Long Beach. In 1970 she was awarded the National Prize at the Eleventh International Festival of Painting at Cagnes-sur-Mer (France), and in the following year obtained an open grant from the Canada Arts Council. She has produced diverse interior and exterior murals at Toronto, New York, Dallas and Washington. Her works are found in many public and private collections.

SELECTED BIBLIOGRAPHY

1958   Jacques Folch-Ribas, dans *Vie des Arts*, Vol. III, No 13, p. 54.

1961   Pierre Saucier, *Jeunes artistes au travail*, in *Vie des Arts*, Vol. V, No. 22, p. 39.
        Claude Beaulieu, *Rita Letendre*, dans *Vie des Arts*, Vol. VI, No 25, p. 54.

1963   Jacques Folch-Ribas, *Rita Letendre*, dans *Vie des Arts*, Vol. VIII, No 33, p. 70.

1966   Guy Fournier, *Une expérience murale de Rita Letendre*, dans *Vie des Arts*, Vol. X, No 42, p. 61-62.
        Letendre et la vitesse des masses colorées, in *La Presse*, Montreal, October 15.

1969   Normand Thériault, *Rita Letendre: La Marche lumineuse*, in *La Presse*, October 11.
        Claude-Lyse Gagnon, *Rita Letendre*, in *Vie des Arts*, Vol. XIV, No. 57, p. 57.

1971   Catalogue of the *Rita Letendre* Exhibition at the Galerie de Montréal. Introduction by Gilles
            Hénault, 12 pages.

1972   *Autour du soleil*, in *La Presse*, November 11.

1974   Catalogue of the *Rita Letendre* Exhibition. Articles by various critics; Palm Springs Desert
            Museum, Palm Springs, California, 32 pages.

1975   Rita Letendre, *Rita Letendre, peintre*, in *Maclean*, March, pp. 26-27, 50 and 52.

1976   Catalogue of the *Vibrations colorées de Rita Letendre* Exhibition, Montreal Museum of Fine Arts.
        Robert Smythe, *Arrows of Energy Softened with Spray Gun*, in *The Ottawa Citizen*, November 13,
            p. 53.

MOLINARI

Ghislain CLERMONT

What I value most in Guido Molinari's painted work is that it is remarkable in its unity, its strict and continued development, the clarity and logic of its language. The catalogue that Pierre Théberge recently wrote for the National Gallery of Canada (*Guido Molinari,* 1976) describes Molinari's development, the evolution and growing influence of his style. From 1950 to 1954 he felt his way, associated with the Automatists, signers of the *Refus global* and propagandists of free painting. Molinari tried his hand at the spontaneous gesture and thick paint. In 1955 he settled down and produced black and white pictures. Three years later he became enthusiastic over hard edge and returned to colour. At the end of 1963 he took up equal vertical bands. He seemed unable to get enough of them, so that he is identified with them and this is said of him in no uncertain terms. The former protester of La Hutte (1951-1953), the former director-founder of L'Actuelle Gallery (1955-1957), the former guru of the Plasticians and of the Non-Automatists (from 1959-1960) was, in 1968, accused by younger artists of being set in his ways. The following year, the parallel bands were ended and a new phase, of checks and triangles, began.

With Molinari the word is on a par with the gesture. Great steps are marked as much by justificative commentaries as by swings in the conceptions of the works. Molinari has always loved — and still greatly loves — talking (to artists, to critics, to the curious, to his own pupils as well as to those of others) and writing (in newspapers, in periodicals, in exhibition catalogues). This is how the twenty-seven texts compiled and presented by Pierre Théberge with his catalogue on the retrospective (*Guido Molinari: Écrits sur l'art, 1954-1975,* 1976) are a little mine to be exploited. Upon reading these various statements, spread over a period of twenty-two years, I tried to understand what Molinari himself called *molinarism* in 1954, even before defining it.

One might say that molinarism rests on three basic precepts. First, it is exclusively abstract: "Abstract painting is the predominant element in contemporary pictorial activity" (*Écrits,* p. 22). Molinari reproaches figurative painting with limiting the artist's dynamic and expressive possibilities, because it remains a slave to tradition through the realistic perception of objects and their perspectivist organization in space. He places value on the abstract method, *the only authentic one,* and gives it great merit. It allows the artist to deviate from the illusory dualism inherent in the figurative method, the act of placing on plane surfaces objects in an environment. It also permits him to join a new objectivity of the real, to closely examine its structure and then to develop an expressive, personal language.

Molinarism is fundamentally the linking of the destiny of painting to an evolution of the structure of space: "The first plastic reality resides in structure, that is, in the dynamic function resulting from the relationship between elements, colour and plane" (p. 18). In 1955, in his very first article, Molinari connected the evolution of his painting to the future of the new plastic, which rejects the Euclidian perspective (illusionist) and natural space (classical). He accuses his former Automatist friends, his former associates at La Hutte, of remaining attached to space in three dimensions and to accidents considered as objects. From whence arose the necessary break with Cubism and Surrealism, retrograde and still attached to volume and plane. It was the Cézanne-Mondrian-Pollock filiation that must be respected, it was Mondrian who must become the model: "This is how a very definable evolution exists from Cézanne to Pollock, which consists of the progressive destruction of volume and plane in the space of the picture. Mondrian, for his part, destroyed the plane-object determined through light-evaluation and he introduced the dynamic plane where colour finds all its energetic possibilities" (p. 17). In Mondrian, Molinari finds "the Plastician, the objective, impersonal artist", a bold step which had, however, "delighted" Borduas in March 1944. But Borduas spoke of fine light and space, and Molinari prefers Mondrian's theoretical bases to his images. This is extraordinary: a young Quebecer not thirty years old who, oddly, knows with whom to compete in the matter of abstract painting! Certainly, Molinari likes Mondrian very much, but he also wishes to outstrip him, he wishes to break with the impression of distance, of gravity and of the lateral that is still found in the work of geometric abstraction's founder.

I like the ascetic series of black and white pictures of 1955-1956. *Angle noir* (1956, National Gallery of Canada) is typical Molinari in this respect. Molinari freed of all automatism becomes Molinari the intellectual, the geometrician, the purist. Now he has it, his new structure of space: the forms and the background are reversible, the pictorial field is bidimensional. Twenty years later, at the University of Quebec at Montreal, he would define, as a university professor sometimes knows how to define things, what he had understood since the fifties as plastic structure, as expressive structure: "The term structure . . . designates a particular way of tackling the phenomenon of *totality* formed by the pictorial work and a fashion of understanding it in its components, emotive as well as conceptual . . . The structure which constitutes the picture is naturally formed by its elements, but the laws of composition of these elements are not only additive or cumulative. The laws of composition attribute to the whole as such properties of the whole distinct from those of the elements taken each by itself. A picture is not only the sum of its elements, but it is the synthetic outcome of the interrelations between those elements" (p. 99).

It is amazing to realize that, in the middle of the fifties, Guido Molinari, practising the highly abstract method in Montreal and Alex Colville, working in the highly figurative method in Sackville, N.B., were both absorbed in an existential painting. Bernard Teyssèdre, who lived with these canvases, says of them: "One can see in them a *tragic* way of living" (Canadian Cultural Centre, Paris, *Guido Molinari,* 1975, p. 8).

Colour came back, however. At the end of 1958 vertical bands began to dance. They were coloured: white and black, red, orange and yellow. Later there would be blue and green, and sometimes brown. This was (also) pure colour used as a structural element, like energy (not like light). Colour and plane — the two fundamental words in molinarist language —

were combined; colour and form as well. Molinari said it once and for all in 1972 to those clever men of the Canadian Society for Colour in Art, Industry and Science: "In art, one cannot find or experience colour as such, but only form-colour units interrelated with other form-colour units to create a specific, meaningful experience" (p. 86). For Molinari this experience is first lived by the artist: the artist communicates a message "which cannot be other than that of lived experience". Forms and colours make one, they create the structure of the painted work, they make a new being — the picture — born of a particular experience of a particular artist at a particular moment.

To accomplish this colour-plane and colour-form unity, a particular development, a precise analytic method are necessary. Whence arises the third precept of molinarism: the organization of the picture according to certain constants, or again the complex, systematic utilization of arrangement in series. In fact Molinari wishes to produce the synthesis between the dynamisms of duration and the dynamisms of colour. To do this, he believes that only arrangement in series allows: a) avoiding that one colour polarizes the whole picture; b) giving a dialectical function to a colour by repeating it or relocating it in the picture; c) ridding oneself, by the repetition of always identical forms, of the traditional dualism of colours (dark or light, warm or cold) and forms (linear forms or masses, large or small forms); d) eliminating the effects of texture, roughness, over-finishing, which restrain dynamism and the expression of colour (see text 23 of *Écrits*).

Guido Molinari's work is an extension of that of the founders of abstraction. Molinari has derived much from Mondrian and Malevitch. He has also reacted strongly to Pollock, De Kooning and Kline. His research is parallel to Noland's and Newman's. In Canada the controversial aspect of his development is toning down. Molinarism has entered into our history of painting.

GUIDO MOLINARI   BIOGRAPHICAL NOTES

Guido Molinari was born in Montreal in 1933. He studied at the Montreal School of Fine Arts and at the Art School of the Montreal Museum of Fine Arts, under Marian Scott and Gordon Weber. In 1953 he founded and directed Galerie L'Actuelle, the first gallery in Canada to concentrate exclusively on non-figurative art. With other abstract artists, he participated in the *Espace 55* exhibition at the Montreal Museum of Fine Arts in 1955. From 1967 to 1968 Molinari was vice-president of the Association of Professional Artists of Quebec and a member of the International Society of Experimental Aesthetics. An associate in 1965, he was elected a member of the Royal Canadian Academy in 1969. He taught at the Art School of the Montreal Museum of Fine Arts from 1963 to 1965 and is presently a professor at Concordia University. His works are to be seen in large public and private collections in Canada and abroad.

SELECTED BIBLIOGRAPHY

1958   Jacques Folch-Ribas, *Les Calligraphies de Guido Molinari*, in *Vie des Arts*, Vol. III, No. 13, p. 54.

1964   Claude Beaulieu, *Guido Molinari*, in *Vie des Arts*, Vol. IX, No. 37, p. 51.

1965   Claude Jasmin, *Toccate et fugues de Molinari, Hurtubise et Tousignant sur des airs connus*, in *La Presse*, Montreal, May 29.

1972   Laurent Lamy, *Molinari, une intransigeante pureté formelle*, in *Vie des Arts*, Vol. XVI, No. 66, pp. 53-57.

1974   François Laurin, *Les Peintures en damiers de Molinari*, in *Journal of Canadian Art History 1*, pp. 35-39.

1975   Céline Bengle, *Évolution picturale de l'œuvre de Guido Molinari*. Master's thesis at the University of Montreal, 260 pages.
        A Study Concerning the Dyads, Multiple Squares Structures and Triangular Compositions Created by Molinari in the Years 1969-1970. Master's thesis at Concordia University, Montreal.
        Guido Molinari. Introduction by Bernard Teyssèdre. Canadian Cultural Centre, Paris.

1976   Guido Molinari, *Écrits sur l'art, 1954-1975*. Edited by Pierre Théberge. Documents on history of Canadian art, No. 2, The National Gallery of Canada, Ottawa.
        Guido Molinari, Catalogue by Pierre Théberge, The National Gallery of Canada, Ottawa.
        Alain Parent, *Molinari ou la construction d'un espace*, in *Vie des Arts*, Vol. XXI, No. 83, pp. 38-40.
        France Morin and Chantal Pontbriand, *Entrevue avec Guido Molinari*, in *Parachute*, No. 4, pp. 31-36.
        Gilles Toupin, *Guido Molinari ou le langage de la couleur*, in *La Presse*, November 27, p. E24.
        François-Marc Gagnon, *The 'Precociousness' of Guido Molinari*, in *Artscanada*, Toronto, Nos. 210/211, December-January, pp. 55-58.

PELLAN

Gilles DAIGNEAULT

In ancient Greece, they gave the name of rhap-
sodes (that is, *sewers*) to itinerant singers who *adapted* elements of
different sources and dialects in their recitals. Homer was just
one of these rhapsodes, but his name has come down to us because
his poetic genius was able to give to a traditional material a new
form and a new spirit and transform an amalgam of motley
fragments into a work of art which, in spite of inevitable *errors,*
still speaks to us.

Now, the pictorial adventure of Pellan — this
truculent Quebecer of Catalan, Scottish and Norman ancestry,
Parisian by adoption during the good years — who assimilated and
re-thought the writings, however diverse, of most of the *ism*
movements that followed each other in France from 1905, presents
a certain analogy with Homeric poetics. In fact, in the manner
of the rhapsodes Pellan has *sewn* into his pictures elements borrowed from Fauvism, Cubism, Surrealism, Tachism, etc., but in
Homer's fashion he has created a universe that intelligently in-
corporates these borrowings and that is striking, not only by the
power of its poetry but most often by its coherence and its
originality. No doubt Pellan will laugh at this comparison between
his work and the Greek epic, but this will only add strength to my
argument, for it is precisely his laugh, sonorous and contagious
like the laughter of the gods, that first called forth for me the
image of Homer (which I later sought to present in a more academic way).

Be that as it may, if one visits Pellan with the
hope of learning more about his pictorial conceptions or better
knowing the functioning of his plastic thought, one takes a great
risk of coming away disappointed: "Have you seen my 1972
retrospective? Then you know everything. I don't need to talk . . .
Besides, I am not so good at it." Having said this, the man is
very kind and he is willing to "chat awhile about it". However, one
quickly regrets having insisted upon this. Indeed, Pellan only tells,
without too much conviction, about things he has already repeated
a hundred times; it is not his fault, critics have so little imagination! We are familiar with his remarks on the importance of the
production of pictures, of *perception,* of drawing, on the vibrations of colours, etc.; his outbursts on "easy painting", on Breton,
on "pure" abstract art, on . . . Borduas, etc. Briefly, at first sight,
nothing that really *advances the discussion.* And yet, when later
I saw again a few of Pellan's too-rare pictures visible in Montreal
in normal times[1], I felt that these two hours spent at the artist's
could have a certain importance, although they seemed like
nothing.

It has sometimes been said that Pellan's house is related to his pictures, and even if the artist says that he always creates each of them slowly and deliberately, this one, that he has never finished retouching for almost thirty years, will surely be the work in which he will display the greatest part of his fantasy and his dreams. And, even if he does not hesitate to declare — in agreement, for once, with Borduas — that he could continue his work anywhere, "even in Tierra del Fuego", it seems almost as difficult to imagine to-day a Pellan creating away from this home *that possesses him,* as one of his girls frolicking outside of the *Piscine de jouvence.* This incorrigibly youthful house that now calls to mind a laboratory, now a playroom, is the crucible of Pellanian creation and when visiting it one believes one is at the same time in a little museum and a large picture. Then one begins to imagine the enchantment that a big museum devoted to this work would offer, and Pellan does not like to see his works leave ("It's somehow like our children . . ."). He regrets, however, that several of them are seen by only a few individuals and will confess without false modesty that he also dreams of a place where they would all be collected together. "Unfortunately, we wait for artists to die to do that sort of thing . . ."

For the moment, Pellan is very much alive, and just his physical presence constitutes an important cog in this universe that recalls the one that Miró created in the gardens of the Maeght Foundation, where forms and colours seem to draw their freedom in an imagination like that of children. I referred above to Pellan's "Homeric" laughter; we must also speak of his eternal youth, this other attribute that he gives the impression of sharing with the gods. Nothing is left untouched by the baths of youth he imposes on his environment: stone masonry, painter's palettes, shoes, pebbles, agates, etc. are transformed into so many elements literally emerging from his pictures, that enchant him as much as they do us. And when we see him in the midst of his creation, we tell ourselves that basically Pellan is himself *a* Pellan. Therefore, as with his pictures, it is advisable to look at him and let him talk. And, like his pictures, his laughter carries echoes of the mad Parisian escapade and his eyes are filled with delightful *Water Fairies,* one in particular. As for the rest, Pellan remains, still in the image of his work, a fabric of attractive paradoxes. Under the circumstances, a meeting with the artist therefore allows better penetrating the work, not as a source of explicit commentaries, but, in some way, as an integral part of this work.

After all, what can be said to-day of Pellan's work? Let us say right now that, for reasons beyond his control, the painter has been obliged to considerably slow the rhythm of his work during the last years, and that it is rather difficult to bring an enlightened judgment to bear on the recent variations of this writing which, during the Forties, formed a very personal synthesis of varied trends in Parisian art. Pellan's famous "perception" had then come into play and had permitted him to *forage,* in the arsenal of these schools, all that was going to build his style. Thanks to an original temperament strong enough to reconcile opposites and not be submerged by influences, from Fauvism Pellan had retained the idea that pure colours were pre-eminently the means of expression of immediate sensations, but he was reluctant to let himself be dominated, like some Fauves, by the expressive power of these colours. Pellan then became interested in the intellectual development of the Cubists, but this energetic colourist could not hold to the pictorial austerity to which this strict, lucid approach most often led. And if Pellan is indebted to Surrealism for having opened his mind to unexplored poetic or fairy-like worlds, he has always challenged the competence of a Breton in the matter of painting and, certainly, his authoritarianism in all other matters; on the other hand, he had already paid too much attention to the plastic value of the elements used in his pictures to accept the demands of the Surrealists on the subject of the primacy of the contents. This great concern for purely plastic values would incidentally have pushed him toward abstraction if a profound need "to humanize all this" had not possessed him (Pellan would drolly say of his stone masonry that it was an *abstract work* before he transformed it into a bestiary).

None of that was the result of intellectual work. Pellan questioned the research of others only to better withdraw into himself and through these different pictorial adventures it was the life of painting itself that he observed and the working of his own plastic thought of which he had an inkling. In fact, as soon as he had the feeling of having found his writing, he would completely stop concerning himself with what was being done elsewhere in painting and would find inspiration only in his own resources. Hardly would his work sometimes be coloured by elements borrowed from Quebec craftsmanship, or Indian or Eskimo art. But the main point is that Pellan would no longer deal with anything but images and forms that carried his mark, while trying to carry further and further his arabesques and his transformations. It has been written that the painter gave of his best during his Paris period and that he later remained cut off from the future of painting. Well, Pellan, whom criticism does not annoy too much (it would fascinate him rather in his good moments), is convinced he has attached himself to the future of his *own* painting. As for the rest . . .

All things considered, Pellan's universe appears to us as an inexhaustible reservoir of beautiful images, of an astonishing subtlety, capable of developing in the attentive viewer a sort of sensuality of vision that helps him to better grasp the *terrestrial foods.* And, if we remember that in ancient Greece they learned to read and to think only from the *Iliad* and the *Odyssey,* it is regrettable that to-day we cannot easily have access to Pellan's work to gather from it by the handful an art of living . . . and of laughing.

---

1. Note the recent acquisition by the Museum of Contemporary Art of *Mascarade,* an invigorating picture of 1942, of surrealist inspiration, which had been very much noticed at the Panorama I Exhibition organized by Gilles Hénault, about twelve years ago.

ALFRED PELLAN   BIOGRAPHICAL NOTES

Born at Quebec in 1906, Alfred Pellan was a pupil at the Quebec School of Fine Arts from 1922 to 1925. First holder of a Province of Quebec scholarship, he lived in Paris from 1926 to 1940 and studied at the École Supérieure Nationale des Beaux-Arts, then at the Academies of Grande-Chaumière, Colarossi and Ranson. Upon his return to Canada, he settled in Montreal and taught at the Fine Arts School from 1943 to 1952. He was awarded first prize in painting at the Spring Exhibition (Montreal Museum of Fine Arts) in 1948. In the same year he signed the *Prisme d'Yeux* manifesto. Recipient of a grant from the Royal Society of Canada, he again resided in Paris from 1952 to 1955. A retrospective of his works was presented at the National Museum of Modern Art of the City of Paris in 1955. In 1971 he became a member of the Royal Academy of Canada. In 1972, a large retrospective exhibition of Pellan's works was presented at the Montreal Museum of Fine Arts, at the Quebec Museum and at the National Gallery at Ottawa. Also in 1972 he received the Philippe-Hébert Prize awarded by the Saint-Jean-Baptiste Society of Montreal. In 1974 a doctorate honoris causa (letters) was conferred upon him by the University of Montreal.

Pellan has produced many theatrical costumes and décors, and murals in paint, glass, ceramic and fluorescent paint. His works are found in several public collections, both in this country and abroad.

SELECTED BIBLIOGRAPHY

1941   Jacques de Tonnancour, *Alfred Pellan, propos sur un sorcier*, in *Amérique Française*, Vol. I, Nos. 2 and 3, pp. 34-40 and 53-55.

1943   Maurice Gagnon, *Pellan*. L'Arbre, Montreal.

1945   *Cinquante dessins d'Alfred Pellan*. Éditions Lucien Parizeau, Montreal.

1946   Robert Ayre, *Pellan versus the Band*, in *Canadian Art*, Vol. III.

1951   Geoffrey Drayton, *Canadian Rebel: Alfred Pellan*, in *The Studio*, London.

1955   Jean Cassou, Pellan Catalogue, Musée National d'Art Moderne, Paris.
Joe Plaskett, *Paris Honours Alfred Pellan*, in *Canadian Art*, Vol. XII, No. 3.

1958   Bernard Dorival, *Trois peintres canadiens au Musée National d'Art Moderne de Paris*, in *Vie des Arts*, Vol. II, No. 10, pp. 19-29.

1959   Paul Toupin, *Pellan chez lui*, in *Vie des Arts*, Vol. IV, No. 17, pp. 31-36.

1960   Paul Gladu, *Mes tableaux, ce sont mes inquiétudes*; Alfred Pellan catalogue, The National Gallery of Canada, Ottawa.

1962   Donald W. Buchanan, *Alfred Pellan*. McClelland and Stewart, Toronto.

1963   Guy Robert, *Pellan*. Éditions du Centre de Psychologie et de Pédagogie, Montreal.

1966   Russell J. Harper, *Painting in Canada*. Toronto University Press.

1972   Germain Lefebvre, Pellan catalogue. Montreal Museum of Fine Arts; *Saison Pellan*, in *Vie des Arts*, Vol. XVII, No. 68, pp. 48-53.
Jean Bédard, *La Sauvagerie apprivoisée de Pellan*, in *Culture Vivante*, No. 26.
Catherine Bates, *Quebec's Alfred Pellan still Leads the Artistic Pack*, in *The Montreal Star*, October.

1973   Germain Lefebvre, *Pellan*, Les Éditions de l'Homme, Montreal; McClelland and Stewart, Toronto.
Pellan. Éditions Yvan Boulerice, Montreal.
Alfred Pellan retrospective at the Quebec Museum. Press clippings scrapbook, 141 pages.

1974   Reesa Greenberg, *Surrealism and Pellan: L'Amour fou*, in *The Journal of Canadian Art History*, Vol. I, No. 2, pp. 1-11.

1975   An interview, *Alfred Pellan, témoin du surréalisme*, in *Vie des Arts*, Vol. XX, No. 80, pp. 18-21.

1976   Reesa Greenberg, *Surrealism Traits in the Heads of Alfred Pellan* in *Journal of Canadian Art History*, No. 3, pp. 55-72.

1977   André-G. Bourassa, *Surréalisme et littérature québécoise*, Éditions L'Étincelle, Montreal.

RIOPELLE

Virgil G. HAMMOCK

Jean-Paul Riopelle is a Canadian artist like Alex Colville who enjoys a solid international reputation and like his realist colleague he can afford to be above the nitty-gritty of Canadian art politics. I have been lucky enough to have had long discussions with both artists over the past year. It is safe to say that nearly the only thing that these artists have in common is their fame, but it is Riopelle that I am concerned with here.[1] It is correct to say that Riopelle is better liked, even known, outside his native Quebec than within. Whether this is due to his long artistic exile in France or the professional jealousies of some of his less successful Quebec colleagues begs the question. It should be remembered, however, that Jean-Paul's successes are his own and the result of hard work.

Riopelle came of age during World War Two. This was a period of artistic and cultural repression in Quebec. Controlled on one side by the conservative policies of Maurice Duplessis' Union Nationale Party and, on the other side, by the even more conservative Catholic church, avant-gardism didn't have much of a chance in Quebec. Riopelle showed his artistic talent at an early age when he took special art classes for children at the Montreal Museum of Fine Arts school under the guidance of Arthur Lismer. From there he enrolled at the École des Beaux-Arts, but he was soon, during the fall of 1942, drawn into the École du Meuble and the teaching of Paul-Émile Borduas. This early contact with Borduas cannot be over-emphasized. Riopelle and his fellow followers of Borduas were, like their teacher, under the spell of Surrealism — a school which was nearly in exile in North America during the war. Surrealism was at the root of both the Automatistes, the name that the Borduas group coined for themselves, and the Abstract Expressionist movement in the United States.

To talk to Riopelle is to recall the very beginnings of modern abstract painting in Canada. It is difficult to believe that Riopelle, once considered to be the 'enfant terrible' of Canadian art, is now approaching his middle fifties. He was in on the start of it all — in Quebec, New York and Paris. His friends are, or were, in the forefront of modern art history. Frank O'Hara, the late, sainted poet laureate of Abstract Expressionism, called him ". . . one of the most important figures to emerge in the School of Paris since the end of World War II and probably the most important artist in Canada's history"[2]. I am sure that Jean-Paul would deny the School of Paris label — at least he has done so to me — and the second view is a matter of opinion, but one to be reckoned with.

Soon after Riopelle joined Borduas' group, the young artist's work was shown with that of other disciples including Pierre Gauvreau, Fernand Leduc, Françoise Sullivan and Jean-Paul Mousseau, in a series of small exhibitions in Montreal organized by Guy Viau, who was himself a Borduas student, and his brother, Jacques. It would be difficult to say what, if any, influence these very early exhibitions of Riopelle and his fellow Automatistes had on the history of Canadian painting, but they predate similar efforts to show abstract work in Toronto, and elsewhere in Canada, by several years. Certainly the Montreal group's work was known by some artists in Toronto, but the Toronto of the Forties was an even more conservative place than Montreal, which is saying quite a bit. Art in Toronto at this time was still in the strangle-hold of the dictates of the Group of Seven and their immediate successor, the Canadian Group of Painters.

The war was hardly over when, in 1946, Riopelle set off for Paris. He knew that there was much to be learned and seen outside Quebec. He knew that his art would be better accepted elsewhere. He thought, with some justification, that to stay in Quebec tilting cultural windmills would prove futile. It would sap his energies just when they needed stimulation. History has proven him correct. How many of those artists who exhibited with Riopelle in the Forties, have survived with anything like the reputation he now enjoys? It is interesting to try and figure out why Jean-Paul has never become a particularly strong influence on other Quebec artists. It could be simply that he left Quebec at an early age — he was, after all, in 1946, but twenty-three — and that he had neither the time nor the experience to make an impact. He hasn't, however, like other Canadian artists, both English and French, who left Canada to seek their fortunes, returned from time to time to propagandize his position, but has continued to live, in the main, in exile.

I doubt if there are many people in Canada who realize that Riopelle has a Canadian studio. I didn't. It is located at L'Estérel in the Laurentians. A friend and I spent the better part of an hour driving up and down a narrow road in Sainte-Marguerite before we found it. The studio is a large, comfortable three-storey building designed by the artist, that sits high on a large sloping lot overlooking a lake. It is built so that one enters the building over a short bridge-line deck into the top floor, which serves as a spacious painting studio. The bottom floor opens at ground level and there is a path to a dock on the lake where a float plane is tied. The plane is piloted by Riopelle on some of his hunting trips. Living quarters — kitchen, dining, living, bath and bedroom areas — are on the second floor, the lower level being a drawing studio and additional living areas. It is all pretty deluxe and a long way removed from a humble hunting lodge or garret studio, but why not? Riopelle has style — this is where, to me, he is his most European. His trips to Canada, however, are not to see museums, but to hunt and fish in our northern woods.

It had been five years since I had last seen Jean-Paul and I was anxious to see if he had changed. He hadn't. Except that we were both five years older. We soon fell into a conversation about our common passion — automobiles — Bugattis, Ferraris, Bristols; the main difference is that he can afford the real thing and I only read about them. At least there is one area where we remain equal. We are both left handed! I had been invited to lunch. The lot that Riopelle's studio is located on is large and he shares it with a long-time friend, a Montreal doctor, who has also built a home on it. It was the doctor's wife who prepared the meal and a real North American menu it was — Arctic char, caught on a recent fishing trip, corn on the cob, a small salad, fruit, cheese and much wine. It was after lunch that I settled into a comfortable chair and continued my conversation with Riopelle about his work and development.

It is subject matter that links Riopelle from the start to Canada, however abstract some of the work might appear to the casual viewer. He is obviously aware of this relationship. In the drawing studio I had a chance to see a series of his most recent works on paper, some destined to be used as a basis for serigraphs, based on his hunting trips in the North. They were of vast flights of birds blanketing the skies over remote lakes and woods, or of hunting camp scenes. They are more representational than most works that are usually associated with the artist, but they are unmistakably Riopelles.

There is no denying, however, that there is a self-conscious space in the artist's work that can be related only to the Canadian experience. Riopelle remains a North American painter with more than just a touch of post-war European elegance. He fell under the influence of American painting just at the time when it was emerging as the most powerful force in the art world. He first visited New York in 1946, but he returned in 1949 to spend a year in the city or rather East Hampton where Jackson Pollock's studio was located. It was during this period that he came to know the American artists who made New York the world centre it was: Kline, Pollock, De Kooning, Motherwell and many others. Much has been written on the subject of Pollock's influence on Riopelle, both pro and con, but to my mind, and after talking to Jean-Paul about it, I think that Pollock's influence was no more than that of any number of artists of the American school. Riopelle told me that the first time he met Pollock was at the famous Cedar Bar. Jean-Paul was with Franz Kline, who introduced them. Pollock talked only about cars and not a word about art. The two artists later became good friends. Pollock even visited Riopelle in Europe, but without a doubt the American artist that Jean-Paul admired most was Franz Kline and not Pollock.

The American critic Harold Rosenberg called certain Abstract Expressionists 'Action Painters' and this term is certainy appropriate to Riopelle. The credo of the Automatistes was action not only in painting, but social action as well. It is interesting, the form that painting took both in Canada and in the United States during the late Forties and early Fifties, a period of general political repression. In the Thirties, American painting had concerned itself with social realism — left wing idealism, but after the war, during the so-called 'Cold War', the Abstract Expressionists turned inward, making individual rather than group statements. In Quebec, on the other hand, the Automatistes issued a group manifesto: the *Refus global*. This 1948 bombshell, with the title essay by Borduas and a cover illustration by the young Riopelle, was a call to arms for Quebecers. It urged them to cast aside the conventions of church and government in the name of art. It was a brave act that was to ruin Borduas' artistic life in Quebec. Riopelle was, however, by this time already committed to living in France.

There is a popular conception that Quebec art in the Forties and Fifties owed more to France and the School of Paris than to contemporaneous American or English Canadian models. Riopelle would deny the European influence, with the exception of the already mentioned Surrealism, and although he was not directly influenced by the Abstract Expressionists while a student, their art certainly helped shape his first mature works. It is hard to say what effect the early visits to New York and Paris had on Riopelle, but in my opinion he certainly got the scale for his large pictures from the Americans. It is, after all, the large scale which gives the Abstract Expressionists a great deal of their power — or better still their grandeur — and this is where Riopelle stands apart from his fellow Automatistes.

I started out by saying that the only thing that Riopelle and Colville had in common was their fame. However, another thing that they do have in common is the fact that I don't think that either one of them could have ever been called avant-garde, at least in the sense that the word is commonly used. In fact, nearly fifteen years ago, in 1963, Riopelle was called *The Young Old Master* by Philip Pocock in an article in *Canadian Art* (now *Artscanada*). He said, in part, that: "His (Riopelle's) dedication is not the old game of 'flabbergasting the philistines' but to creative work whose lasting qualities are best seen by considering some aspects of 'up-to-the-minute' painting. Later in the same article he wrote: "This is a labour of love and joy — not the visual extension of hatred and rage. Long is the list of the positive attributes of Riopelle's work and it is a list which adds up and equates to an intensive affirmation of reality."[3] Both of these points are as true to-day as they were in 1963. The work I saw in Riopelle's studio was joyful and full of energy. While it is true to say that Riopelle is, and was, a painter of nature, it would be a mistake to think of him as a 'Rousseauian' man subservient only to nature. Riopelle is the master and not the servant of nature. Nature has been a powerful force in Canadian art history, almost smothering everything else, as was the case in the Group of Seven. Jean-Paul is very aware of both art and art history as well as his place in it. He is one of the most sophisticated artists I have met and it is this sophistication that lends credence to his view of nature.

If Riopelle had not painted a single picture since 1962, the year that he won the prestigious Unesco award at the Venice Biennale representing Canada, the fact would still have to be faced that he was the first Canadian artist to attain world stature. He is still working and to my mind making important pictures which will be remembered long after many of the fads of the current Canadian scene are forgotten.

1. For my discussion on Colville see: Virgil G. Hammock, *Alex Colville: Perfection and Reality*, in *Vie des Arts*, Vol. XXI, No. 84, pp. 86-89.

2. Frank O'Hara, *Riopelle: International Speedscapes*, in *Art News*, Vol. 62, April 1963, p. 32.

3. Philip Pocock, *The Young Old Master*, in *Canadian Art*, Vol. 20, March 1963, p. 113.

4. See: Michael Greenwood, *Jean-Paul Riopelle: Poet of the Sign*, in *Artscanada*, Vol. 28, August-September 1971, pp. 66-68.

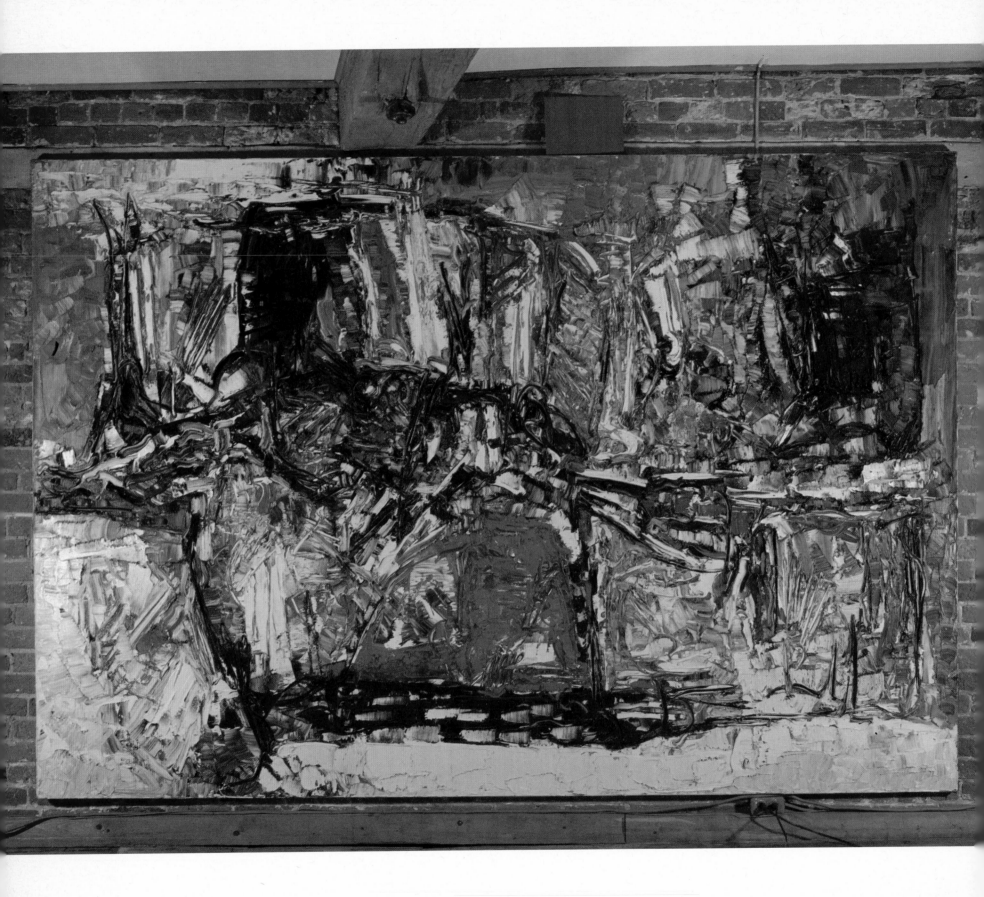

JEAN-PAUL RIOPELLE   BIOGRAPHICAL NOTES

Born in Montreal in 1923, Jean-Paul Riopelle studied at the Montreal School of Fine Arts, then at the École du Meuble in 1943-1944. He frequently visited the studio of his professor, Paul-Émile Borduas, joined the automatists and exhibited with them, for the first time, in 1946. That same year he went to Paris and to Germany, and participated with Barbeau, Gauvreau, Leduc and Mousseau in the international surrealists' exhibition in New York. In 1948 he signed the manifesto titled *Refus global* before finally settling in Paris, where he carved out an international reputation for himself.

In addition to painting, Riopelle has produced since 1966 important engraving work, notably several lithographs published in *Derrière le miroir* by Maeght Editeur, as well as some drawings of leaves and animals, among which are his famous owls. Since the beginning of the sixties, he has also taken up sculpture; he has produced several small bronzes and some monumental works. In 1976 he created *La Joute*, a sculptural composition evoking the flag game and intended for the Olympic site at Montreal.

He received an honourable mention at the São Paulo Biennial in 1955, and a mention at the Guggenheim International Prize Competition in 1958. Riopelle represented Canada at the Venice Biennial of 1952 and there received the Unesco Prize. In 1973 the Saint-Jean-Baptiste Society awarded him the Philippe-Hébert Prize. The University of Sherbrooke has recently bestowed on him on honorary degree.

The name of Jean-Paul Riopelle is seen in great anthologies of modern art and his works are part of important public and private collections, equally in Canada and abroad.

SELECTED BIBLIOGRAPHY

1952   Georges Duthuit, *Painter of awakening, Jean-Paul Riopelle*, in *Canadian Art*, Vol. 10, No. 1.

1956   P. Heron, *Exposition Riopelle à Gimpel Fils Gallery, London*, in *Arts*, New York, No. 30.
        Pierre Schneider, *Jean-Paul Riopelle*, in *L'Oeil*, Paris, No. 18.

1957   Guy Viau, *Le Prix national Guggenheim*, in *Canadian Art*, No. 15.

1960   *Derrière le miroir*, Galerie Maeght, Paris, No. 160.

1962   *La Sculpture de peintre: Bronzes de Riopelle*, Jacques Dubourg, de Paris, 12 pages.

1963   Jean Cathelin, *Jean-Paul Riopelle*, in *Cimaise*, No. 66.

1964   R. H. Hubbard, Preface for the catalogue of the *Canadian Painting 1939-1963* Exhibition at the
        Tate Gallery, London. The National Gallery of Canada, Ottawa.
        Guy Robert, *École de Montréal, Situation et tendances*. Montreal, Éditions du Centre de
        Psychologie et de Pédagogie (*Artistes Canadiens* Collection).

1965   André Breton, *Le Surréalisme et la peinture*. Gallimard, Paris.

1967   *Riopelle*, Quebec Museum, 53 pages.

1968   Jean Sutherland Boggs, Preface for the catalogue of the *Canada, Art d'aujourd'hui* Exhibition,
        Musée National d'Art Moderne de Paris, January-February.
        Derrière le miroir, Galerie Maeght, Paris, No. 171.

1970   Guy Robert, *Riopelle, ou la poétique du geste*, Les Éditions de l'Homme, Montreal.
        Derrière le miroir, Galerie Maeght, Paris, No. 185.

1971   Henry Galy-Carles, *Borduas et les automatistes au Grand-Palais de Paris*, in *Les Lettres
        Françaises*, Paris, October 6.

1972   Pierre Schneider, *Riopelle, Signes mêlés*. Maeght, Paris, 175 pages.
        Riopelle, ficelles et autres jeux, Canadian Cultural Centre, Paris, 42 pages.

1974   Gilles Toupin, *Jean-Paul Riopelle: Un cheminement de 25 ans en 36 tableaux*, in *La Presse*,
        Montreal, May 25, p. E1.

de TONNANCOUR

Gilles HÉNAULT

Recently I saw Jacques de Tonnancour in his studio on a sunny afternoon (miraculous after the long, rainy September weeks).

My first impression on entering: Am I in an artist's studio or in an entomologist's study? Only a few canvases are on the wall: one reads like a lost alphabet; another flatly displays an immense crab on the canvas; on others, smaller, evanescent fish fossilize in a stone grisaille. Everywhere there are collections of beetles, butterflies, scarab beetles, spiders, cicadas, in short, of insects whose shapes and multicoloured spots are set according to species. There are also Indian drawings (as beautiful as paths in the forest) that inscribe their symbols on bark as thin as papyrus, beside strange necklaces from Amazon tribes or elsewhere. Voyages have left their relics or residues there.

De Tonnancour explains to me. A few months ago he had an exhibition and now he is waiting. It is "input" that engrosses him at this time, much more than "output". I have in front of me a man who uses a language of the 20th century, a refined, cultivated man, an artist who has *succeeded,* but whose transparency is only seemingly apparent. I discover that he is obsessed by a passion of his childhood, haunted by insects and by their proliferation in tropical jungles. So in his speech there appears a barbarous poetry, in a flight of diurnal and nocturnal butterflies. Some of these are already placed on the canvas in the shape of bluish dreams.

In a *flashback* I again see young De Tonnancour, who, more than thirty years ago, exhibited canvases inspired by his *anxiety* in the face of Matisse and Picasso, this Picasso himself troubled by the discovery of negro masks, by an archaelogy which was to shake all contemporary art, so true is it that man, like civilization, must search time in all its dimensions to preserve an equilibrium: not a return, but a recourse to childhood or to the fertile wonder of the great primitive myths.

Some painters evolve quickly. De Tonnancour is not among them. After his first portraits and his still lifes in the manner of . . . (a young artist is always influenced by someone, and that's normal), he was to try to re-orientate himself, to place himself pictorially in an experienced context, in a relationship with nature. And he would paint a whole series of landscapes. At the beginning, Goodridge Roberts' influence was felt in these canvases, but this influence would be toned down as De Tonnancour would move more deeply into "the forest of symbols" to discover his own language there.

Suddenly I became a film maker and I saw the development of his work (because there are the individual canvases that are grouped in a large movement to utter a definitive phrase, an expression of the artist's very step in his research on an equivalence to the mystery of the world) and I made a zoom that showed me the tree as sign (because if we say we cannot see the forest for the trees, the contrary is still more true: the forest hides the trees from us). These signs evolved toward pictograms, and, like what we see in Chinese art, showed me the general in the particular.

Then occurred a reversal of the process, as if the artist had been afraid of losing contact with the material. Next came the series of collages. In reality, the effect of enlargement continued; it showed trees as texture, rugosity, space where the eye no longer recognizes the sign but the bark with its roughness, its luminous variations, its sores and its planes, its coloured fields.

Then, danger appeared. It was necessary to show again that art is not nature, that the spirit of geometry is certainly man's own. (However, this doctrine is ambiguous, because everywhere nature lavishly sows its theorems in shells, its insect symmetries, its cubism in crystals). De Tonnancour would take this into account, for his natural bent led him to favour form; he would therefore compose his pictures by inscribing his personal stroke on a gritty background; I mean his own geometry, his writing.

More Pascalian than he believes (or, perhaps, does he know it?), De Tonnancour is always torn between the spirit of finesse and the spirit of geometry. To-day we shall use other words to express this phenomenon: the psychiatrist would speak to us of the subconscious and the conscious; the anthropologist of the primitive and the civilized; the linguist of the significant and the signified. But with the artist, these forces are always arranged on the basis of the sign to be produced, the symbol to be invented.

If I continue my zoom, I observe that there are insects on the bark. De Tonnancour tells me that, when looking at a tree, he instinctively sweeps it with his eye to discover insects, *ideograms* inscribed on the tree and, most of the time, camouflaged, like characters of ancient writings on bamboos, tablets or palimpsests.

New elements of a pictorial language, from that time on they entered into the composition of the painting. The painter had to take possession of them in order to transform them into stylized forms, into blobs and lines, like fossilized elements that leave only their unnatural, therefore artificial, prints, art being also artifice. And, indeed, De Tonnancour showed me stones containing fossils, of which some of his canvases are plastic evidence, that is, transposed.

I well realize what can be arbitrary in this kinetic analysis of the evolution of an artist and his work. However, this method is no stranger to the fact that, thanks to modern techniques, De Tonnancour was able to project in front of me a series of slides that formed a certain retrospective of his painting. The reconstruction of a step that is spread over many years cannot be made in a systematic fashion. An artist's personal development is never shielded from the global evolution of the history of art, nor, particularly, from special *accidents* that can guide properly pictorial research in an unexpected direction. Thus, De Tonnancour did not hide from me the fact that it was by chance, while using stamping procedures, that he was led to orientate himself toward collages.

In the same way, it was while spraying paint of a special blue on a canvas that he established a relationship with the blue of the wings of an Amazon butterfly, which gave birth to the series of pictures of insects. So it is from his own plastic language that De Tonnancour evolved, that he assembles forms and colours, and that he reorganizes them.

Will the form of the insect dissolve in the colour of blobs with contours at the same time supple, unforseeable and often symmetrical (an astonishing balance between the spirit of delicacy and that of geometry), in De Tonnancour's future production? Will the insect-sign become purely pictorial surface, as previously the tree-sign of the landscape became blended with its bark? No one can say, not even De Tonnancour, because his development does not conform to a programme. At present, he is shopping, assimilating, travelling, accumulating sensations. Insects *devour* his painting, or rather mobilize his attention and invade his poetic space.

This wait would perhaps be hopeless if it were not the recovery of a childhood passion, a discovery of poetry and a possible paradise through photographs in the *National Geographic Magazine,* whose pages De Tonnancour has leafed through hundreds of times where, for all through life, individual mythologies are born.

He confided to me that at the time he wanted to become an entomologist, but that since he did not believe he was gifted in the sciences (and yet his scientific vocabulary in this domain fascinates me), he had decided to enter the School of Fine Arts, to learn to . . . draw insects!

Having graduated from the School, he no longer searched for "the little beast"; he entered the great adventure of pictorial research. At the time of his first stay in Brazil, immediately after the war, it was the passion for painting that haunted him. But now, when he goes to the sources of the Amazon, or when he penetrates into the jungles or Peru, Bolivia or Panama, De Tonnancour leaves on the butterfly hunt of his childhood, he pursues his dreams of coleoptera, in a true poetic safari. From those places he brings back admirable specimens and slides evocative of a world like the Garden of Eden, where Indian tribes lead an autonomous life and have very ambiguous relations with *tourists.*

In his elegant apartment in Côte Sainte-Catherine, this Indian presence is discreetly displayed in a few drawings on beaten bark. But the signs of another consuming interest appear in the form of shells. These are not real collections; rather an assembly of strange geometrical, multiform tombs (from a marine cemetery?). De Tonnancour refuses to become involved in the devilish cycle of collecting that Jean Baudrillard explains in *Le Système des objets,* where he says, in particular, that La Bruyère, in the portraits in which he illustrates curiosity as a passion, describes to us a collector of prints: "I have," he says, "a sensitive affliction that obliges me to give up prints for the rest of my life: I have all of Callot, except one, which is not really one of his good pieces of work. On the contrary, it is one of his lesser works, but the one which would complete my Callots. I have been working for twenty years to obtain this print, and I finally despair of succeeding; this is very hard on me."

I was saying, therefore, that it is not in this frame of mind that De Tonnancour *collects.* One ought rather to think that he *gathers* what delights him or what astonishes him. If he assembles objects, it is "for the pleasure of the eye", as the sellers in Moroccan bazaars nicely say.

If there is a constant in De Tonnancour's work, or a basic design, it is drawing, the form as intelligence of a nature that continues to amaze him by the strangeness of its inventions. "This is a joke of nature!" he exclaims in the face of the *harlequin* beetle.

"Two fundamental literary qualities: supernaturalism and irony," Baudelaire wrote. I believe that De Tonnancour would accept that his art should be defined in these terms, adding to this a certain archaelogy of knowledge.

I cannot end this article in any other way than to quote a few lines from Valéry's *Cimetière marin,* a poem of which the artist is particularly fond:

> Having come here, the future is laziness.
> The clean insect scratches dryness;
> All is burned, undone, received into the air
> Like some unknown sharp perfume . . .''

JACQUES DE TONNANCOUR   BIOGRAPHICAL NOTES

Born in Montreal in 1917, Jacques de Tonnancour studied at the Montreal School of Fine Arts from 1937 to 1940. From 1942 to 1952, he taught at the Montreal School of Art and Design. He wrote the *Prisme d'Yeux* manifesto in 1948 at Montreal. Since 1954 he has been a professor at the Montreal School of Fine Arts which was later integrated into the University of Quebec at Montreal. In 1957 and 1959, he was given the purchasing award at the Biennale of the National Gallery of Canada. He was honoured with a second prize at the Artistic Competitions of the Province of Quebec in 1963 and 1968. He produced the mural for the Dow Planetarium in Montreal in 1966 and in 1969 created a series of integrated sculptures and murals for the University of Montreal. Jacques de Tonnancour's works appear in the important public and private collections of Canada.

SELECTED BIBLIOGRAPHY

1943   Jacques G. de Tonnancour, *Remarques sur l'art*, in *Amérique Française*, Nos. 2 and 3, pp. 34-40 and 53-55.

1958   Rodolphe de Repentigny, *Les premières expositions de 1958*, in *Vie des Arts*, Vol. II, No. 10, p. 42.

1964   Jacques Folch-Ribas, *De Tonnancour*, in *Vie des Arts*, Vol. IX, No. 35, p. 52.

1965   M. Ebbitt Cutler, *Artist in Perspective: Jacques de Tonnancour*, in *Canadian Art* No. 22, pp. 36-38.

1966   Catalogue of the *Jacques de Tonnancour, 1942-1965* exhibition. Preface by Jacques Folch-Ribas, Montreal Museum of Contemporary Art, 16 pages.
Catalogue of the *Jacques de Tonnancour* exhibition; introduction by Richard Simmins and Doris Shadbolt, The Vancouver Art Gallery, 30 pages.

1969   Normand Thériault, *De Tonnancour: Une peinture intimiste*, in *La Presse*, Montreal, March 29, p. 33.

1970   Normand Thériault, *De Tonnancour: Je suis anachronique*, in *La Presse*, October 31, p. D 14.

1971   Jacques Folch-Ribas, *Jacques de Tonnancour, le signe et le temps*. L'Université du Québec Press (Studio Collection).
Jacques de Tonnancour, *Dumouchel — L'Homme*, in *Vie des Arts*, Vol. XVI, No. 64, pp. 13-16.

1975   Henry Lehmann, *De Tonnancour Speaks*, in *The Montreal Star*, November 1, p. D-5.

TOUSIGNANT

Laurent LAMY

When Tousignant began to paint in 1952, what was he confronted with? The innovation made by automatist painting went back ten years, around Borduas' gouaches titled *Abstraction*. A break was finally made with all that formerly existed in Quebec, and the break was well accomplished: Tousignant was able to profit from Borduas' experience. *Representation* was challenged, but not pictorial space, since the automatists always retained the presence of forms on a background, of signs more or less related and existing in a perspectivist space. In the United States, during the fifties, action painting artists were engaged in an automatism of another kind; for them, painting was actualization, immediate experience. Abstract Expressionism therefore defined the pictorial context when Tousignant came out of the School of the Museum of Fine Arts in 1951 after three years of study with Weber, who was very knowledgeable about contemporary art, and toward whom Tousignant feels a certain gratitude for having "opened his eyes"[1]. Toward the end of 1952, Tousignant left for a short stay in Paris. In May 1953, he was back in Montreal. To-day, he considers that the influence of the School of Paris held him back in his development toward attaining a "pure and evident"[2] painting.

At that time, Molinari was directing the Galerie de l'Échourie that presented the painting of the first group of Plasticians made up of Jauran, Belzile, Jérôme and Toupin, but also the works of the Automatists. In their manifesto (1955), the Plasticians termed the Automatists' revolution "germinal"[3] but, for them, the plastic facts were to constitute an end in themselves. In the same year, Tousignant presented at l'Échourie an exhibition of tachist canvases, exploiting pictorial space in the American *all over* that eliminated the landscape space of the Automatists. Tousignant would follow a route parallel to that of Molinari, with whom he would have contact and constant exchanges.

From 1956 he worked in search of a minimum spatiality by occupying the surface of the canvas with two or three very much contrasted coloured planes. His choice showed great courage: at that time, hard edge was badly received by the public and even by the automatist painters. Reduction, simplification and negation led him to radically change his language, to recognize as primordial the spatial quality of colour. Two 1956 canvases illustrate this period well: *Oscillation,* whose surface is divided vertically into two equal black and red zones, and *Frontale,* in which a narrow vertical band contrasts with the blue-back mass on the right. The bidimensionality of the canvas, clearly asserted in a *dynamic* imaginary space born of the coloured surfaces, commands attention in no referential or perspectivist aspect. Tousignant broke with the first generation of Plasticians who, in the direct line of Cubism, had confined themselves to grayish, dull colours. The power of saturated colour already took an "essential"[4] part in Tousignant's problem.

The use of bright colours and of the oblique line established coloured relationships on quasi-vertical planes or on angled planes and participated in the monumentality of colour as well as in the affirmation of the surface.

Wishing to treat colour as object and ridding it of everything that is not colour, through simple geometric forms, Tousignant drew from chromatic relations a maximum impact.

From 1963 on appear circular surfaces situated now at one side of the picture, now at the other, sometimes at the centre, creating a tension with the square or rectangular surface of the picture which acts as support: the strongly coloured circle asserts itself in a well defined space and the borders of the canvas are emphasized by coloured bands of different widths. The circular surface having a tendency to occupy more and more space, Tousignant subdivides it into concentric circles that finally invade the whole canvas, as in *Ad absurdum* or *Oeil-de-bœuf,* pictures of 1964 that he calls "targets". The gaze strikes these circles opening out toward the exterior like waves and breaks on the borders of the canvas. The reading is interrupted and opposed. Tousignant already felt this confrontation was an impasse when two sides of the square coincided with two sides of the rectangular surface of the picture. But when concentric circles take their place in orthogonal pictures, the much increased confrontation is so strong that it curbs the visual expansion of the circles and limits the sensation of fullness aroused by them.

Tousignant found the solution in the harmony between container and contents: the inoperative corners[5] of the picture having been eliminated, the concentric circles entered into a circular picture-support. In this way, one of the preferred and decisive moments of Tousignant's pictorial trajectory blossomed out in the series *Transformateurs chromatiques* (1955), *Gongs* (1966) and *Accélérateurs chromatiques* (1967). A fruitful period if there ever was one, which made Tousignant known in Canada and abroad. A success that makes sense only if it is put back in its place following the period of development that preceded it. Even if he refused all allegiance to Op Art, Tousignant no less participated in its world consecration since he was represented in the Responsive Eye Exhibition at the New York Museum of Modern Art in 1965. It is certain that the intentions of the Op painters are different from Tousignant's.

Experimentation and exploitation of the different chromatic values and diversity in the dimension of circular bands permitted numerous optical effects that Tousignant considers secondary. They exist, however. It is important that it should be the canvas as a whole that becomes a vibratory field of colours. The circles lose their formal identity to become only chromatic supports.

Composed, at the beginning, of three or four wide concentric bands in contrasting colours, the pictures were later constructed of bands two inches wide, then a half inch, and finally a quarter inch. Simutaneously, the number of colours increased, going from two to three, to four . . . alternating colours. Through the multiplication of optic effects and chromatic vibrations, the notion of surface disappeared, was lost. In another development, the canvas was subdivided into wide zones which themselves were subdivided into very narrow bands of different colours. From there Tousignant exploited variants of the process by regrouping the same colours into narrow bands in order to make them more operative. Thus, in *Gongs* the optical mixture of bands of the same colour a quarter inch in width on a wide zone of another colour creates a third colour floating on the surface, which plays in its turn with the adjacent vibrant zones, doubly putting *the canvas into action*. A movement, centrifugal and centripetal at the same time, animates the canvas all the more because the colours, of an intense luminosity, set off quasi-stroboscopic flashes.

In the third development, that of *Accélérateurs chromatiques,* Tousignant exploited a new structuralization of the canvas by the repetition of identical or inverted, opposed or interpolated series. The structure of colour in series by bands of equal width and equal values then took precedence over the optical vibrations and the chromatic relationships were much increased. In the repetition of a series of seven colours, for example, the choice and the position of each of the colours gave rise to an organization so complex that it is with difficulty perceptible: the structure in series, that is felt rather than really perceived, escapes the eye because, at the moment one believes he possesses it, hop, op! it is rebuilt in another fashion, instigating an infinity of readings. By gradual elimination Tousignant arrived at visual affirmations of a great simplicity of form but of a remarkable chromatic richness. The analogy of his disks with the magic circle (mandala), figure of serenity, harmony and equilibrium, supports and motivates the pleasure of undoing and redoing the combining play that forms the picture.

In 1969 the concentric circles were stretched horizontally and became ovals or ellipses. The eye followed the trajectory of the colour by a back and forth reading that, at the ends, followed the curves of the semi-circles.

In a next development, Tousignant eliminated the horizontal part of the oval between the two semi-circles that he completed and connected in space, which opened on a number of chromatic relations of a different order from those previously explored. The reading of the two circular canvases cannot be carried on otherwise than from one to the other. The colours reversed or shifted from one element to the other oblige the production of varied visual paths, each element being discerned in itself, then in its relation to the other. Appreciation takes place in the united vision, inseparable from the elements of the diptych, as in the case of *Le Bleu et le noir 1972*, composed of two large blue and black circles. There is an identity of form (circle and ring) intellectually perceived, but partially contradicted visually by the displacement of the colours: the blue ring of one of the canvases becomes a *blue-circle* in the other; while the black circle becomes a *black-ring* in the other.

At the same time, Tousignant did not abandon his research on the oval. He created his *Diagonales* composed of very long oval elements in concentric bands, hung in a slanting position on the wall. In the compositions formed of this type of element, possibly reaching as many as eight in number, there is an acceleration of the moving of colour as in a cascade. Through the repetition of the following procedure — a partial resumption of a series from which he removed one colour to replace it with another — there is established a flight of spiralled, circular reading with neither beginning nor end. A whole language, founded on the series composed of variables obtained by additions and subtractions, has been put in place, with what the exploitation of a system at the same time entails and reveals of fixity and openness.

In 1973-1974 Tousignant produced *canvas-sculptures* formed of unequal vertical modules whose top ended in a semi-circle. Placed on the ground, increasing in height, these modules of a single colour form a triangular ensemble, each part of which acts like a band participating in the whole, in the same way as in the pictures of the sixties. The semi-circle pictures sixteen feet in diameter, standing on their diameters on the ground, also show the continuity of the research all directed on spatial intervention by the dynamics of colour and the suppressing of the picture's frame.

Even if Tousignant has always said that he has never had any other ambition than "to bring painting to its source, where nothing is left but the painting emptied of everything that is foreign to it, where painting is only feeling"[6], a point of view shared by many contemporary artists, can we thus separate the impression received by the eye from the socio-cultural environment in which it dwells? And can "feeling" be isolated from emotionality, from intellect? Ambition is high and most severe when the painter desires that his painting express nothing but itself. But leading us to perceive the complex and even learned disposition of coloured surfaces, forcing us to active participation, making us enjoy the energetic force and lyricism of colour, all this is part of Tousignant's work. He invites us to a genuine education of the eye, a transformation of the gaze and the milieu that welcomes it. The monumental character of his works contributes to making us feel how much this production, in its obstinacy in exploiting only the circle, in its severity and in its superb clarity, compels recognition to-day by its coherence. Painting of pure picturality? Certainly not.

1. Interview with Laurent Lamy, September 27, 1977.
2. Claude Tousignant, *Text Anti-Text*, in William Withrow, *Contemporary Painting*, Toronto, McClelland and Stewart Ltd., 1972, p. 137.
3. *Manifeste des plasticiens*, in *Jauran et les premiers plasticiens*. Museum of Contemporary Art catalogue, Montreal, 1977.
4. François-Marc Gagnon, *Claude Tousignant point de mire* in *Vie des Arts*, Vol. XVII, No. 69, p. 38.
5. In his concrete language, Tousignant calls these dead corners "ears".
6. Quoted by Danielle Corbeil in the introduction to the *Catalogue of the Claude Tousignant Exhibition*, 1973-1974, National Gallery of Canada, Ottawa, 1973, p. 8.

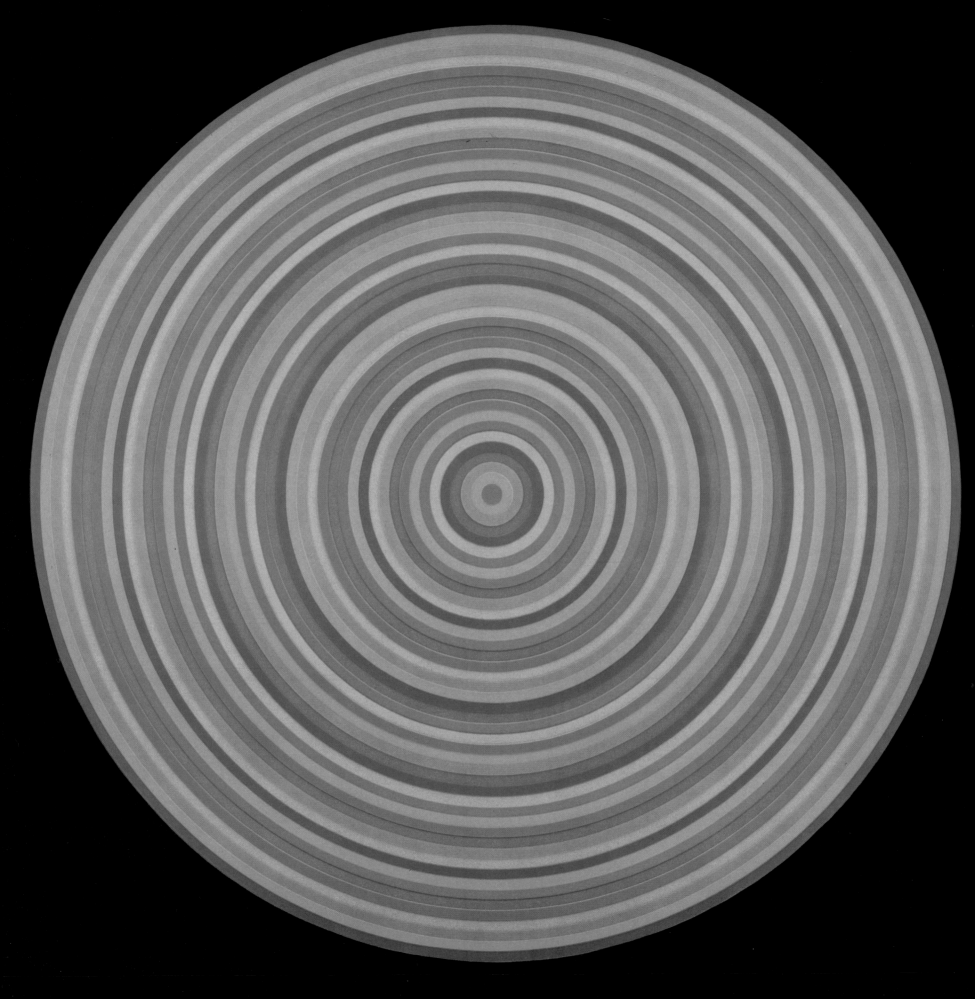

CLAUDE TOUSIGNANT   BIOGRAPHICAL NOTES

Claude Tousignant was born in Montreal in 1932. He studied at the Montreal Museum School of Art and Design from 1948 to 1952 under Arthur Lismer, Jacques de Tonnancour, Louis Archambault, Gordon Weber and Marian Scott. He lived in Paris in 1952 and 1953, attending l'Académie Ranson. In 1962 he won first prize at the Salon de la Jeune Peinture, and in 1967 first prize in the painting division of *Perspectives 67* at Toronto. Tousignant is particularly known for his pictures in circular form, successively called targets, gongs, chromatic transformers, chromatic accelerators; with Molinari, he was one of the chief artisans of the dispute between automatism and the development of plastician intentions. In 1973 a Claude Tousignant retrospective was presented at the National Gallery of Canada in Ottawa; in the same year he won the prize of the Canadian Institute of Rome. His work is represented in many museums, abroad as well as in Canada.

SELECTED BIBLIOGRAPHY

1965   Claude Jasmin, *Toccate et fugues de Molinari, Hurtubise et Tousignant sur des airs connus*, in *La Presse*, Montreal, May 29.

1966   Fernande Saint-Martin, *Claude Tousignant*, in *Vie des Arts*, Vol. XI, No. 44, p. 46.

1968   Yves Robillard, *La Sculpture, planche de salut des plasticiens*, in *La Presse*, March 9.
1969   Normand Thériault, *Un cercle qui n'est plus rond*, in *La Presse*, May 10, p. 46.

1971   Claude Tousignant, *Quelques précisions essentielles*, in *Peinture canadienne-française* (Débats). Université de Montréal Press, Montreal.

1972   François-Marc Gagnon, *Claude Tousignant, point de mire*, in *Vie des Arts*, Vol. XVII, No. 69, pp. 38-43.

1973   *Claude Tousignant*. Introduction by Judith Terry and essay by Fernande Saint-Martin. Éditions Yvan Boulerice, Montreal.
       Claude Tousignant. Introduction by Danielle Corbeil; The National Gallery of Canada, Ottawa.
       Luc d'Iberville Moreau, *Claude Tousignant*, in *Artscanada*, No. 30, pp. 51-55.

1976   Henry Lehmann, *Activated Spaces*, in *The Montreal Star*, May 22, p. D5.
       Walter Klepac, *Claude Tousignant*, in *Artscanada*, No. 206/207.

BIOGRAPHICAL NOTES ON THE AUTHORS

Jean-Loup Bourget

After teaching at the University of Toronto, Jean-Loup Bourget became cultural attaché at the French embassy in London, then at the French consulate in Chicago. He is presently cultural attaché at the French embassy in New York. He contributes regularly to *Vie des Arts,* as well as to the film magazine *Positif,* to *Jazz Magazine* and to the *Times Literary Supplement.*

Monique Brunet-Weinmann

Born in 1943 in Ollioules, France, and living in Montreal since 1969, Monique Brunet-Weinmann was a teacher of French at the Rosemont CEGEP, then lecturer in comparative aesthetics in the Faculty of Literature and Aesthetics at UQUAM. She has also taught at McGill University and at the University of Ottawa. She held grants from the Government of Quebec and the Canada Arts Council, and is a member of the Art Association of Canadian Universities.

Ghislain Clermont

An instructor in art history at the Department of Visual Arts, University of Moncton, Ghislain Clermont is a former director of the University art gallery. He studied at the University of Montreal and the University of British Columbia.

Gilles Daigneault

Born in Montreal in 1943, holder of a Ph.D. in Greek studies, for lack of students in this austere discipline Gilles Daigneault was obliged to teach linguistics and literature. At present he is writing a monograph on Léon Bellefleur and conducting research on Quebec engraving.

Florence de Mèredieu

Born in Paris in 1944, Florence de Mèredieu holds a teaching diploma in philosophy. Since 1970 she has been assistant lecturer in Plastic Arts at the Teaching and Research Unit at Paris I (Panthéon-Sorbonne) and, since 1975, full professor at the National Centre for Tele-Education (Vanves), University Education.

Jean-Pierre Duquette

Born in Valleyfield, Quebec, in 1939, Jean-Pierre Duquette holds a Ph.D. in French literature. He is presently a professor in the Faculty of French Language and Literature at McGill University.

François-Marc Gagnon

Born in Paris to Canadian parents in 1935, a bachelor of philosophy (University of Ottawa, 1965) and doctor of history of art (Sorbonne, 1969), François-Marc Gagnon was a teacher at the Montreal School of Fine Arts from 1960 to 1965. Since 1966 he has been a professor in the Faculty of History of Art at the University of Montreal.

Virgil G. Hammock

President of the Canadian section of the International Association of Art Critics (IAAC), Virgil G. Hammock is a professor in the Fine Arts Faculty at Mount Allison University, New Brunswick.

Gilles Hénault

Journalist Gilles Hénault was director of the arts section of *Le Devoir* from 1959 to 1961. Having contributed to several magazines, he is a co-founder of *Liberté* magazine. As script-writer or animator, he has also taken part in many radio and television broadcasts and has edited adaptations for the National Film Board. Director of the Museum of Contemporary Art from 1966 to 1971, he was later advisor in museology to the Quebec Ministry of Cultural Affairs for a year. He is presently assistant lecturer in literature at the University of Quebec in Montreal.

Laurent Lamy

Born in Montreal in 1929, Laurent Lamy contributes to several newspapers and art magazines, both Canadian and foreign. In 1967 he founded the Canadian Section of the International Association of Art Critics (IAAC) and represented Canada at a number of international conventions of this association. Since 1960 he has frequently taken part in broadcasts on the arts on Radio-Canada radio and television; since 1970 he has contributed to the radio programme *L'Art, aujourd'hui.* In 1975-1976 he was director of the Visual Arts Sector of COJO'S Programme *Arts et Culture.* He is a professor in the Fine Arts Department of the Old Montreal CEGEP.

Germain Lefebvre

Born in Montreal in 1941, Germain Lefebvre holds a master's degree in arts from the University of Montreal. He has been a member of the staff at the Montreal Museum of Fine Arts since 1968, and, until recently, held the position of assistant curator in charge of the Department of Canadian Art. He is now working for the Provincial Administration.

Bernard Lévy

Director of *Chercheurs* magazine, the periodical on research activities at the University of Montreal, Bernard Lévy is a graduate in sciences (physics, chemistry and biology) and in letters (history). He has a professional education as editor and journalist. He is a member of the editorial staff of *Vie des Arts.*

Micheline Moisan

An art historian and a museologist, Micheline Moisan is curator of the drawings and prints department at the Montreal Museum of Fine Arts since 1976.

André Parinaud

Born at Chamallières, France, a reporter for thirty years, in the press, on television and on the radio, André Parinaud is presently director and executive editor of the French magazine *Galerie-Jardin des Arts.*

Gilles Rioux

Having received an education in history of art, Gilles Rioux considers his activity as critic the natural complement to the instruction provided in some Montreal institutions.

Guy Robert

The first director of the Montreal Museum of Contemporary Art in 1964 and winner of the literary Grand Prix of Montreal in 1976, Guy Robert is very active in the artistic world. At the same time art and literary critic, poet and aesthetician, he is the author of numerous articles published in magazines and newspapers, as well as of some thirty books, about half of which are devoted to Quebec artists. He also takes part in several programmes on radio and television.

BIOGRAPHICAL NOTES ON THE PHOTOGRAPHERS

Jean-Pierre Beaudin

Born on February 18, 1935, Jean-Pierre Beaudin studied at the Montreal School of Fine Arts and the Montreal School of Graphic Arts as well as at the Hamburger Photoschule in Hamburg, West Germany.

He taught part time at the School of Graphic Arts from 1954 to 1957, at the School of Fine Arts from 1967 to 1969 and at the Institute of Applied Art in 1970. From 1959 to 1966 he was a photographer in the Graphic Arts department of Radio-Canada.

Among his principal projects should be mentioned: at the 1967 World Exhibition in Montreal, photographs for the Quebec pavilion and audio-visual shows for the Jeunesses Musicales pavilion; at the 1970 World Exhibition in Osaka, murals for the Quebec pavilion; at Mirabel airport, for the press room, a photographic mural on aluminum measuring 8 feet by 24; for the 1976 Montreal Olympic Games, posters and brochures.

He contributed to the collection of introductory publications on crafts produced by Éditions Formart and has also made for the Quebec Ministry of Education eleven audio-visual creations on the theme of the organization of the enterprise.

Michel Bricheteau

Since 1974, Michel Bricheteau has specialized in photographic reporting on art exhibitions and in setting up photography libraries for artists. Last year he had the opportunity of photographing two exhibitions of Fernand Leduc's work, in Paris and in Brest.

At the same time, he made photographic reports of travels in Egypt, the United States (New York), Greece, Guatamala, Honduras, Italy, Mexico and Turkey.

Gilles Dempsey

Born in Montreal, Gilles Dempsey studied photography in Toronto. Upon his return to Montreal, he participated in several photography exhibitions and in the organizing of *Contact* exhibition. He is presently working on an anthology of Quebec photography from its inception to 1920.

André Maurice

Born at Angers on February 16, 1928, André Maurice plays the cello and the double-bassoon and appeared as an actor in theatre and in the movies. A composer and producer of variety programmes on French television, he has been a producer since 1970.

A friend of Fernand Leduc and connected with the Automatist movement since 1947, he is a painter as well as a photographer.

Gabor Szilasi

Born in 1928 in Budapest, Hungary, Gabor Szilasi settled in Quebec City in 1956. Three years later, he began to work as a photographer in Montreal for the Quebec Film Bureau.

Having received a grant in 1970 from the Canada Arts Council, he produced a photographic essay on the Charlevoix region and Ile-aux-Coudres. In 1973 he took a *photographic* trip to the Beauce; in 1976-1977 an open grant from the Canada Arts Council allowed him to produce a study on the changes in the lifestyle of North-West Quebec.

Szilasi left the Film Bureau in 1972; he is presently a professor of photography at Old Montreal CEGEP and since 1972 has been technical advisor at *Vie des Arts.*

He has exhibited at Montreal, Quebec, Ottawa, Toronto, Vancouver and Chicago. His photographs have appeared in *Arts-canada, Caméra, Culture Vivante, Habitat, Impressions, Ovo, Time* and *Vie des Arts,* and figure in the following collections: Public Archives of Canada, National Gallery of Canada, Montreal Museum of Fine Arts, McCord Museum, Quebec Film Bureau, National Film Bureau, and Mount Allison University in New Brunswick.

Sam Tata

Born to Parsee parents in Shanghai in 1911, Sam Tata took up photography as a pastime in 1937. He spent 1947 and 1948 travelling in India, his parents' country of origin, practising photography. The following year, he returned to Shanghai and recorded photographically the capture of the city by Mao Tse-tung's troops. In 1956 he immigrated to Canada; since that time he has worked full time as a reporter-photo-

grapher for several Canadian magazines and publications, among which are *Time, Weekend, Perspectives, The Montrealer, Star Weekly* and *Canadian Art.*

Basil Zarov

Having begun his career as a photographer with portraits, in 1951 Basil Zarov became interested in the photo-report while producing a work on Arthur Lismer for *Canadian Liberty.* Photographs by him have appeared in *Look, Collier's, Maclean, Paris Match* and *Perspectives.*

Zarov spent three years in Africa to photograph the missions of the United Nations Organization.

He has been president of the Association of Professional Photographers of Quebec.

THE PRINTING OF THIS PUBLICATION WAS COMPLETED
ON SEPTEMBER 12, 1978
ON THE PRESSES OF PIERRE DES MARAIS INC., MONTREAL.
THE TYPOGRAPHY WAS PRODUCED
BY TYPOGRAPHIC SERVICE LIMITED, MONTREAL.
FIVE THOUSAND FIVE HUNDRED COPIES WERE PRINTED IN FRENCH,
OF WHICH ONE HUNDRED PRESENTATION-COPIES ARE NUMBERED FROM 1 TO 100;
AND ONE THOUSAND FIVE HUNDRED IN ENGLISH, OF WHICH FIFTY PRESENTATION-COPIES ARE NUMBERED FROM 1 TO 50.

ALLEYN
BELLEFLEUR
BOISVERT
GAGNON
GAUCHER
GOULET
HURTUBISE
JAQUE
LEDUC
LEMIEUX
LETENDRE
MOLINARI
PELLAN
RIOPELLE
TONNANCOUR
TOUSIGNANT